Multi-Family Therapy

Multi-Family Therapy (MFT) involves the bringing together of different families in a therapeutic context in order to work jointly to overcome each of their specific and very individual problems. This innovative book combines the theory and concepts of MFT with detailed practical examples of techniques and exercises which have been proven to help with problematic children, teenagers and adults.

In this book Asen and Scholz discuss how MFT has been developed over the past 30 years and has been applied nationally and internationally across a range of settings with a variety of clients, including:

- children and teenagers who are excluded from school
- multiproblem families with abuse and violence who challenge social workers and the legal system
- children, teenagers and adults who present with mental health issues.

Multi-Family Therapy: Concepts and techniques is written for professionals in mental health, social work and education. Its unique pragmatic approach makes it an essential guide for anyone wishing to employ MFT.

Eia Asen is a Consultant Child and Adolescent Psychiatrist and a Consultant Psychiatrist in Psychotherapy, and is clinical director of the Marlborough Family Service, London.

Michael Scholz is a Systemic Psychotherapist and the Emeritus Professor of Child and Adolescent Psychiatry and Psychotherapy at the University of Dresden, Germany.

This book captures and makes clear how Multi-family therapy employs an attractive style of always approaching issues through activities that are multiply layered in terms of sensory experiences and also have a lateral/ctrative fun twist, e.g. in work with diverse ethnic groups and different languages having an exercise of babbling (Tower of Babel) in different fantasy languages. The sessions have a feel of being at the circus, the theatre, stand-up comedy, children's party. Above all they transform problems by fun, creativity and humour. A book that is both substantial in its thought and content and also a pleasure and fun to read.

Rudi Dallos, Programme Director of Clinical Psychology, University of Plymouth, UK

In this vividly-written landmark text, Asen and Scholz capture the excitement, creativity, challenges, and effectiveness of Multi-Family Therapy. It is packed with innovative, systematically-based activities readily applicable to working with families in groups or individually. It provides detailed guidance on how to manage the complex group processes that engage families as resources for one another. The authors demonstrate the usefulness of MFT for a wide range of psychiatric and social problems and in a range of institutional settings. For those readers who already practise MFT, this book will expand their repertoire; those new to MFT will be compelled to start a multi-family group immediately. An inspiring, comprehensive book.

Peter Fraenkel, Ph.D. Associate Professor, The City College of the City University of New York & Director, Center for Work and Family, Ackerman Insititue for the Family, USA.

Multi-Family Therapy

Concepts and techniques

Eia Asen and Michael Scholz

Routledge
Taylor & Francis Group

LONDON AND NEW YORK

First published in 2009 as *Praxis der Multifamilientherapie*
by Carl-Auer

This translation first published 2010
by Routledge
27 Church Road, Hove, East Sussex, BN3 2FA

Simultaneously published in the USA and Canada
by Routledge
270 Madison Avenue, New York, NY 10016

*Routledge is an imprint of the Taylor & Francis Group,
an Informa business*

Typeset in Times by
RefineCatch Limited, Bungay, Suffolk
Printed and bound in Great Britain by
TJ International Ltd, Padstow, Cornwall
Paperback cover design by Andrew Ward

British Library Cataloguing in Publication Data
A catalogue record for this book is available from the British Library

Library of Congress Cataloging-in-Publication Data
Asen, Eia, 1946–
    [Praxis der Multifamilientherapie. English]
    Multi-family therapy : concepts and techniques / Eia Asen and
    Michael Scholz.
        p. cm.
    Translation of: Praxis der Multifamilientherapie / Eia Asen and
    Michael Scholz. Heidelberg: Carl-Auer-Verl., 2009.
    Includes bibliographical references and index.
    1. Family psychotherapy.   I. Scholz, Michael, 1941–   II. Title.
    RC488.5.A8413 2010
    616.89′156—dc22   2009051973

ISBN: 978–0–415–55780–1 (hbk)
ISBN: 978–0–415–55781–8 (pbk)

Contents

Figures and tables

Figures

Tables

Preface

Multi-family therapy (MFT) is based on systemic concepts and practices, but instead of working with only one family, many families are seen at the same time. MFT is at times a stand-alone approach, but more often it is used in conjunction with other therapeutic interventions. It has a considerable evidence base in work with children, adults and their families who manifest emotional, behavioural and psychosomatic presentations.

This book aims to inspire professionals working in the fields of health, social services and education, including family therapists, social workers, psychologists, psychiatrists, child and adult psychotherapists, art and occupational therapists, teachers and others working in and with schools.

The approach described in this book was initially created at the Marlborough Family Service in London more than three decades ago and it has since been refined and developed in various different contexts, including in Germany at the Child and Adolescent Psychiatry Department of the University of Dresden. What is presented here is therefore 'work in progress' and invites clinicians to take part in the continuation of this journey. This books aims:

- to provide an overview of recent and current developments in the MFT field
- to introduce professionals working with clients and families who present with emotional and behavioural problems to a new way of working, and to get them to experiment with some of the ideas
- to help professionals already working with MFT to improve techniques and practices
- to interest experienced clinicians in applying the ideas to problems and settings which have to date not been tried and tested
- to describe the innovative ideas and practices of the Marlborough Model and its application in various different work and cultural contexts.

This book cannot be:

- a detailed manual for the treatment of specific disorders or mental health issues
- a comprehensive guide to interventions in the huge field of MFT
- an authentic encyclopedia of MFT projects which colleagues in other countries have developed.

Acknowledgements

This book could not have been written without the sustained help and assistance of the families and teams from London's Marlborough Family Service and Dresden University's Child and Adolescent Psychiatry Department. Many colleagues from both institutions have directly contributed to the ideas and practices described in this book: Neil Dawson, Brenda McHugh, Maud Rix, Beate Schell, Katja Scholz, Dietmar Selig and Derek Taylor. Denise DeRome and Harry Lubasz have helped with making the book more readable. Last but not least, we are very much indebted to Alan Cooklin, without whose vision this model of work would have never been developed.

Acknowledgements

Chapter 1

Concepts and principles

Multi-family therapy (MFT) is anchored in the theory and practice of psychodynamic group and systemic therapy and combines the two. The work in a family group setting is different from traditional single family therapy, as other families and their individual members who experience similar difficulties can provide 'outside' ideas, perspectives and suggestions. It is a common experience that people often find it difficult to be open-minded, let alone objective, about their own situation when in the midst of personal conflict and distress, even though they are well able to be very sensitive and thoughtful about the problems of other people. This phenomenon can be utilized in the work with a group of families if a setting can be created which permits mutual sharing, understanding and transparency. It is a major aim of MFT to enable families and their individual members to go beyond their own perspective(s) and to make use of the many resources that exist in a group setting. Furthermore, families are encouraged to help other families by observing and understanding seemingly identical problems and by making suggestions. Being helpful to others does increase their own feeling of self-worth.

The development of MFT

The practice of working with a number of families together in the same room was first developed in the United States where, during the 1940s and 1950s, several teams experimented with using large group work in the treatment of chronic psychotic patients and their families (Ross 1948; Abrahams and Varon 1953; Kahn and Prestwood 1954). At that time different concepts and formats were used for this work, including psychodrama as well as couple therapy in a group setting (Boas 1962; Gottlieb and Pattison 1966). It is generally agreed that Peter Laqueur is the founding father of MFT. In the 1950s and 1960s he worked in New York with patients with schizophrenia and began to include their relatives in the treatment (Laqueur 1969, 1972, 1973, 1976; Laqueur *et al.* 1964). He soon discovered that well-known dynamics emerged during the course of group therapy, such as joint sharing of experiences, mutual support, constructive criticism and modelling; and all these seemed helpful when families met others who shared similar problems and issues. Relatives who were struggling with specific difficulties with their ill family member soon spotted some very similar themes in other families. Families discovered that they could help each other when exchanging personal experiences, and that they could find different solutions to familiar dilemmas merely by observing how other families managed. Families also provided useful feedback to one another when observing each other interacting. Laqueur's positive results inspired other clinicians, and within a few years various teams of psychiatrists and psychologists developed a number of different approaches, focusing on how to help psychotic patients and their relatives in a larger multi-family context (Detre *et al.* 1961; McFarlane 1982; Anderson 1983). MFT approaches were also developed elsewhere, above all in Europe and South America. Apart from England, teams in France (Benoit *et al.* 1980), Belgium (Igodt 1983) and Switzerland (Salem *et al.* 1985) embraced the approach early on. In Argentina a team had been experimenting since the 1960s with a psychoanalytically inspired MFT approach for the treatment of chronically institutionalized psychotic patients and their relatives (Badaracco 2000).

Over the past three decades many different clinicians and their teams have adapted MFT ideas and techniques to a whole range of problems and disorders (Leichter and Shulman 1974; Hardcastle 1977; Strelnick 1977; Benningfeld 1978; Frager 1978; O'Shea and Phelps 1985). It has become increasingly popular in the field of adult psychiatry: for example, in work with patients with severe depression (Anderson *et al.* 1986; Keitner *et al.* 2002; Fristad *et al.* 2003; Lemmens *et al.* 2007); bipolar disorders (Brennan 1995; Moltz and Newmark 2002); obsessive compulsive disorder (OCD, Barrett *et al.* 2005); substance and alcohol misuse (Kaufman and Kaufman 1979); borderline personality disorders (Berkowitz and Gunderson 2002); bulimia nervosa (Wooley and Lewis 1987); Huntington's chorea (Murburg *et al.* 1988) and other forms of chronic organic illness (Gonzalez *et al.* 1989); as well as in the treatment of chronic pain (Lemmens *et al.* 2005). For the treatment and management of children and adolescents, MFT has proved to be a useful approach, not only in clinical settings but also in schools and social services contexts: for example, in the management of child abuse and neglect (Asen *et al.* 1989); homelessness (Fraenkel 2006); educational failure and exclusion (Dawson and McHugh 1994; Retzlaff *et al.* 2008); eating disorders (Slagerman and Yager 1989; Dare and Eisler 2000; Scholz and Asen 2001; Colahan and Robinson 2002; Asen and Schmidt 2005); children with chronic physical illness (Wamboldt and Levin 1995; Steinglass 1998; Saayman *et al.* 2006); and the wide spectrum of emotional and behavioural disorders (McKay *et al.* 2002). Furthermore, there are many MFT projects which address a variety of disorders or presenting problems, such as Asperger syndrome, attention deficit hyperactivity disorder (ADHD), psychoses, Turner syndrome, family violence and 'out of control' toddlers (Asen 2002; Asen and Scholz 2008).

In England MFT first made an impact in day hospital settings. This first happened in the 1970s, at a time when R. D. Laing's 'anti-psychiatric' ideas (Laing 1960) were still fairly popular, particularly the emphasis on the family being responsible for causing the psychotic presentation of one of its members (Laing and Esterson 1964). The therapeutic community movement (Jones 1968) and various related forms of 'milieu therapy' were additional important models which emphasized how psychological suffering and psychiatric disorders needed to be viewed as being intricately connected with social context. Around this time systemic family therapy took hold and Salvador Minuchin's work with underprivileged and marginalized families, the 'Families of the Slums' was of particular interest (Minuchin *et al.* 1967). All these influences converged when Alan Cooklin, the newly appointed director of the (then) Marlborough Day Hospital in London, decided in 1977 to turn this institution into a systemically oriented clinic working with families and renaming it the Marlborough Family Service. Cooklin and his team were particularly interested in finding innovative ways of working with so-called 'multiproblem families' and this led to the development of a quasi-therapeutic community for these families, the Family Day Unit (Asen *et al.* 1982). In those days the team, with all of its members coming from psycho-analytic backgrounds, had initially few ideas of what to do, other than to interpret behaviour (Cooklin 2001). Parents objected to this and children were too excited to listen to mere words. In the ensuing chaos the team members felt very deskilled, but the families came to our rescue and taught us how to work with them, via trial and error.

Since its inception more than 30 years ago, this paradoxically termed 'institution for change' (Cooklin *et al.* 1983) has undergone several transformations and has inspired many other teams in Europe, North America and Asia and has become a well-established and celebrated model. Salvador Minuchin was very influential in helping the Marlborough team to develop their MFT approach in the late 1970s and early 1980s when he frequently worked there. In those days multi-family work in a day setting, with six to eight families attending whole days for weeks and months, seemed a rather extraordinary if not risky experiment. The Family Day Unit was the first MFT project in England and it inspired the Marlborough Model of MFT (Asen *et al.* 2001) – which is the main focus of this book – as well as many teams all over the world.

Principles of MFT

Much therapeutic work – particularly when it involves children – has developed in settings with clear demarcations between those who provide help and those who receive it. The traditional expert role of doctors, psychologists, teachers, psychotherapists and others implies that it is they who take responsibility for the change process, with parental responsibility often being delegated to staff. The risk is that therapists can sometimes become 'surrogate' parents, particularly if the child also attends a day or residential setting. This may lead to an often unconscious and unintended competition between clinician and parents as to who the 'best parent' is. The paradigm change from child-focused to family-focused work is not easy to make for professionals who have worked for long periods looking after children. However, systemic family work emphasizes that all responsibility for children rests with their parents – even if it is the case that the therapist is responsible for creating the context(s) within which therapeutic work takes place. MFT goes one step further in that it encourages families to be 'therapeutic' to each other, while the therapist attempts to decentralize himself.

MFT combines the advantages of single family therapy with the specifics of group therapy. Group therapy factors (Coughlin and Wimberger 1968; Yalom 1995; Behr 1996), such as mutual support and constructive criticism, role play and feedback are important ingredients of the approach, as is the discovery that suffering is not an isolated experience and that other people may live in similar circumstances. The hope for change, often visible and embodied in other members of the group, is another factor which plays an important role in group work. When considering the multiple interactions and processes that take place simultaneously during group work with families, one could describe these at happening at five levels (Cassano 1989): within families (*intra-family*); between families (*inter-family*); between clinicians, families and their individual members (*therapist–client*); within the large group which is composed of families and clinicians (*intra-group*); and between families, clinicians, the group and the wider context (*extra-group*). In MFT it is the presence of other families with similar problems and difficulties which encourages people to compare notes and help one another to share familiar dilemmas and discuss their respective ways of finding different solutions. Sharing experiences helps families and their individual members to reduce social isolation and overcome the feeling of being singled out or stigmatized, no matter whether this is real or imagined. Families become less defensive when they feel that they are 'all in the same boat' and this leads to a greater degree of openness and to experimenting with being more self-reflective in front of others. This is further enhanced when families also see themselves reflected – or mirrored – in others. In groups families begin to observe each other and they comment on what they like – or dislike – in the way other families manage specific issues. New contacts and connections are made and families develop considerable interest in each other's stories and struggles, the kind of 'curiosity' which Cecchin (1987) described in relation to the stance of the therapist. All this helps families and their individual members to generate different perspectives on seemingly familiar dilemmas. When families are encouraged to voice their perceptions of others – including critical ones – to one another, it is not at all uncommon that their comments or commentaries are often better heard and understood than if very similar observations are made by therapists (Asen 2002).

MFT can be carried out in closed as well as in open groups. It is possible for all families to start and finish together and a closed group is likely to help the development of trust and group cohesion. MFT can also be carried out in open groups, with families leaving and joining at different times and phases of the life of the group. In such a scenario the more experienced families can mentor new arrivals and provide hope – and expertise – from their positions of 'experts by experience'. They may take quite a central role in running groups and thus families become increasingly involved in the process of their own change. This allows therapists to shift from a hands-on to a hands-off stance and to move increasingly to the periphery of what happens. Over time therapists assume the role of 'co-pilots' or, indeed at a later stage, they may resort to taking a 'back seat' (Asen 2006). The rationale for MFT is summarized in Table 1.1.

Table 1.1 Rationale for multi-family therapy (MFT)

- *Creating solidarity:*
  'We are all in the same boat.'
- *Overcoming stigmatization and social isolation:*
  'We are not the only ones with these problems.'
- *Stimulating new perspectives:*
  'I can see clearly those things in them for which, when it comes to us, I am blind.'
- *Learning from each other:*
  'I like the way others manage this.'
- *Being mirrored in others:*
  'We do this just like you.'
- *Positive use of group pressure:*
  'We can't cop out.'
- *Mutual support and feedback:*
  'Terrific how you do this! – and how do you think we are doing?'
- *Discovering and building on competencies:*
  'I can do more than I thought, I am not completely helpless.'
- *Experimenting with 'foster' families and swapping:*
  'We can manage other kids – and I like the way your parents deal with my child.'
- *Intensifying interactions and experiences:*
  'It's like a hothouse, things happen here.'
- *Raising hopes:*
  'Light at the end of the tunnel – even for us.'
- *Practising new behaviours in a safe space:*
  'We can experiment here, even if things go wrong at times.'
- *Strengthening self-reflectiveness:*
  'I can see myself more accurately – and differently.'
- *Promoting openness and increasing self-confidence through 'public' exchanges and interactions:*
  'Nobody is after us, we can open up.'

Therapeutic settings

It is possible to practise MFT in a variety of contexts and locations, from sessional work lasting two hours once or twice per month, carried out in clinics, schools, supermarkets or elsewhere, to work in bespoke institutions such as day units or residential settings. Here between six and eight families may meet for six hours or longer on a daily basis, over weeks or months. It is important to point out that MFT is not only a specific therapeutic tool or method, but also a setting which permits the delivery of other therapeutic modalities, such as single family work, couple therapy or indeed work with just one individual. When families attend for whole days, spontaneous real-life situations and crises tend to arise which can be treated on the spot. Convening therapeutic ad hoc sessions with an individual – be that a parent or child – for perhaps no longer than ten minutes, can be more meaningful and effective than a scheduled 50-minute session a few days later when the heat and intensity have gone. Intensive MFT is a challenge, not only for families, but also for clinicians. As the work is usually highly structured, with tight timetables and frequent transitions from one context to another, family members and therapists need to change their roles and tasks continuously, often within the space of a few minutes. At one point they are members of a large group, a bit later they are 'merely' parents in charge of their children, then members of a parents or children only group, and shortly after one family amongst six or seven other families. These continuous context shifts generate a 'hothouse effect', increasing the pace of change, with staff and families being always 'on the move', having to adopt multiple positions and perspectives.

When in MFT settings families meet other families from different cultures and social backgrounds, this can provoke anxieties, as well as fears of the 'other' and emerging prejudices. Different skin colour, 'strange' languages or dialects, different gestures and mimics, 'foreign' values and beliefs, unfamiliar food and smells – all this can provoke anxiety, distance and rejection. If on top of this interpreters need to be used to overcome language barriers, then the group process can be slowed down and impatience and further intolerance can follow. Despite these initial difficulties during the formation of a group, we have found that intercultural work has a huge potential for families to face the 'other' and the 'alien' and to develop respect for difference. Once families begin to prepare and cook together a multicultural meal where everyone contributes foods and recipes from their countries of origin, they also begin to talk about stories from their native lands. Gradually this also leads to the exploration of difference and in this way MFT can become a form of informal anti-racist training, allowing families to get closer to previously foreign worlds and cultures (Asen 2007b).

A major aim of MFT is to connect families with families and it is the therapist's task to act as a catalyst, making reactions and interactions possible that might otherwise not take place. In order to do so, the therapist cannot merely take a sitting down position, but has to be continuously 'on the move', building bridges between families. As soon as families or their individual members have established some contact, the therapist leaves 'the field'. In this way he signals that families need to get on 'with it' and with each other. The therapist then moves on and mobilizes the next few families. Once this process is set in motion, the therapist can become increasingly less available; he may, for example, offer less eye contact. Many systemic therapists have developed the skill of deliberately not fixing their eyes on just one person, but letting them wander between the different family members. MFT therapists take this further and scan all people in the room, with their eyes moving backwards and forwards literally all the time. This signals partial presence, but at the same time de-emphasizes the importance of the therapist, allowing him to gain and maintain a meta-position. The therapist's increasing distancing tends to have the effect of activating group members to become more active themselves. This may permit the therapist to take some time out and to reflect in (relative) peace on what has been happening and which, if any interventions, to make. It is worth pointing out here that it is not sufficient for therapists to be merely physically 'on the move' – be that with their eyes or with their bodies; therapists also need to be 'on the move' in their heads and minds. This implies an inquisitive stance, characterized by well-meaning curiosity and flexibility, as well as an ability to question in non-threatening ways what is happening between people and what they make of it.

The 'wandering eyes' can be supported by physical actions, for example, when the therapist begins to 'wander' literally between families, or 'orbit', like a satellite, around them. Here the task is to pick up a theme or observation and get members from different families involved in thinking about these: 'Mr P, I noticed that the moment your son John goes over to play with Mary, you intervene. Have I got this wrong? No? It might be interesting to understand why you do this, you probably have good reasons for doing so? Maybe you can talk about this to Mrs G about this?' It is not at all uncommon that in response to such interventive comments, a family or an individual member wants to have a discussion with the therapist, instead of starting a conversation with the member of another family. The MFT therapist, however, does not accept such invitations, but instead redirects the person(s) to communicate with peers: 'Mrs Gluck, please do say the same thing you told me to Mr Peabody, but directly.'

Much of MFT work is 'chairless' – there is no need to sit down, as it were – and is carried out on the move: walking, standing, kneeling down next to a family or individual member. This signals that the therapist is only temporarily available as he metaphorically passes the baton to family members. The therapist is effectively 'in and out' of the action, in a kind of dance routine which is characterized by being both distant and proximal (Stevens *et al.* 1983). He can maybe even leave the room for a while, thereby giving families the message that they have to get on with their 'own thing'. This is not easy initially, as therapists tend to think that their presence, if not central, is nevertheless of crucial importance in any therapeutic ventures. Believing in families' own resources and potential helps the therapist to advance to a more peripheral position and thus allows families to use their own resources and become more self-reliant.

The metaphor of a bird which circles around – maybe even above – the families suggests itself and clarifies this meta-position. From a bird's-eye perspective it is possible to make macroscopic observations and discern inter-action patterns within and between families which would be more difficult to spot from a position right in the middle of the action. When the therapist 'spies' something which seems problematic, he can 'fly' into the problem field and intervene briefly, before taking off again. This way of conceptualizing the therapist's changing positions has been very much influenced by the practice of structural family therapy (Minuchin 1974; Minuchin and Fishman 1981), with its emphasis on detailed observation and enacting problematic scenarios. However, in a multi-family setting it is usually not necessary to stage specific 'enactments', as problematic interactions happen spontaneously and organically. The many different MFT techniques described in the next chapters incorporate playful activities which aim to create or make overt everyday issues that families struggle with.

Chapter 2

Basic techniques

Multi-family work requires multipositional, 'roving' therapists. They need to be able to work on the move, like getting close to families and then distancing themselves, and being able to shift from doing to observing – and back – within very short timespans. Their mindset has to be flexible, rather than following some predecided sequence. During the initial phases of MFT work, the therapists need to make the therapeutic context and take responsibility for it. They have to join with each member of the family from the very beginning and this is best done by starting with an informal role. Light refreshments displayed on a table around which arriving families can congregate provide an opportunity for therapists to mix with families and to engage in non-problem-oriented conversations. Once the formal part of the group starts, it is the therapist's task to create a context that allows for participants to be able to talk and to be heard. If there is a lot of chaos, with screaming and restless children, the therapist asks the parents to control their children, remembering that he is responsible for the context, but that the parents are responsible for their children. It may take a bit of time before the parents succeed with their task, and waiting for this to happen rather than rescuing struggling parents is a more therapeutic stance. It also allows therapists to watch typical samples of potentially problematic intra-family and inter-family interactions and these can be worked with then or later.

At the beginning of an MFT group, therapists often involve themselves in what could be termed 'single family work in the presence of other families'. For example, in a planning meeting (see Chapter 6) the therapist will ask each family in turn how they would want to use the day to address the difficulties and problems that have brought them. Naturally the addressed will respond to the therapist and talk to him. Once this conversation is over, the therapist turns to the next family and asks their individual members a similar question about how to plan the day. In this way the therapist makes contact with each family and involves them in a brief discussion (see Figure 2.1).

However, if communication only flows between the therapist and one family, then other families are relegated to the position of observers of this process rather than becoming directly involved. The therapist therefore attempts to

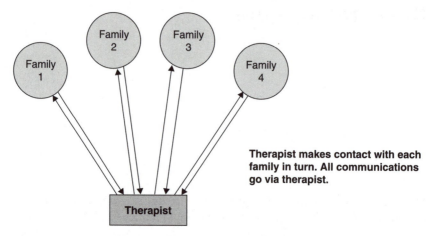

Figure 2.1 Connecting.

draw other families into the discussion: 'Well, so that's what it looks like for the B family – are they alone in thinking that, or are there some other people in this room who have experienced something similar? What do you think Mrs G?' Here the therapist attempts to get a member of another family to comment and to stimulate a conversation around a specific issue or theme (Figure 2.2). He may physically move near these two families and emphasize that both people should have a conversation, without focusing too much on him: 'Maybe you can tell Mrs B directly what you are telling me – and maybe Mr B you could find out from Mr G what he thinks about this?'

When moderating the discussion between the members of two families and standing or kneeling close to them, the therapist is still in a rather central position, actively encouraging them to talk to each other directly. To

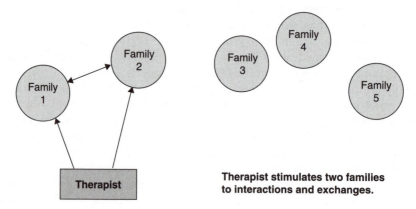

Figure 2.2 Stimulating.

decentralize himself and to fight off the families' natural tendencies to keep him near them and the centre of attention, he can say: 'I know you asked me what I think, but I would be much more interested in what Mr B has to say – after all, he and his family have been in quite a similar situation to yours.' In order to further intensify the interactions between the families (Figure 2.3), the therapist can add: 'Talk to each other, please ignore me . . . pretend I am not here.' To emphasize this point he can get up and move away from these two families.

Once conversations between members of two different families begin, the therapist can leave them to their own devices: 'Keep going, I'll be back, but I want to work with these other families first.' (Figure 2.4) and begin to work with some of the other families present: 'And what is it like for you, Mrs H?'

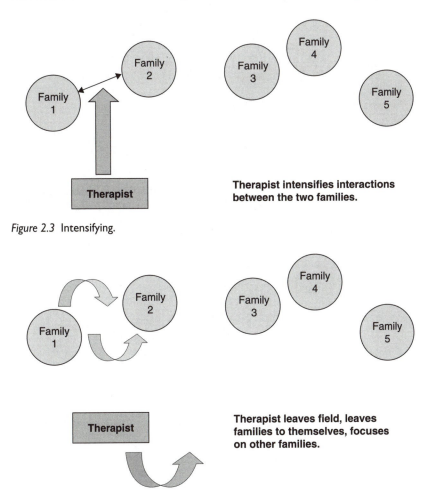

Therapist intensifies interactions between the two families.

Figure 2.3 Intensifying.

Therapist leaves field, leaves families to themselves, focuses on other families.

Figure 2.4 Retreating.

Once the therapist has succeeded in establishing similar contacts and conversations between the members of the remaining families, he can try and connect up the two or three subgroups of families and hope that they will cross-fertilize each other (Figure 2.5): 'I think you are all discussing some quite similar issues – maybe you should all exchange ideas. Perhaps it's best if you form a large circle so that you can discover what is similar and what is different.'

At this stage the therapist is still very central, working with all families actively and acting as a kind of catalyst that keeps things moving (Figure 2.6), so that eventually this gains its own momentum and no longer requires the presence of the therapist.

Once the families are fairly involved in mutual conversations and inter-

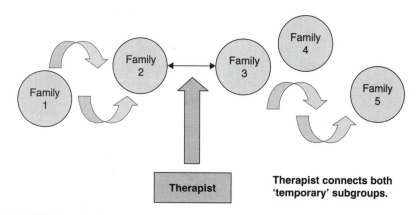

Figure 2.5 Cross-fertilizing.

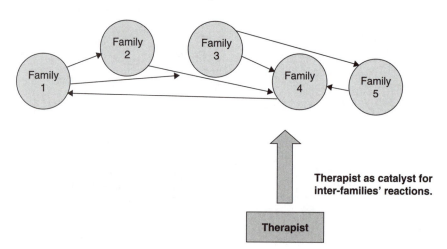

Figure 2.6 Catalyzing.

actions (and this can take the form of them carrying out specific exercises, as described in Chapters 3 to 5), the therapist can move away altogether. He can begin to 'circle' like a bird, perhaps like an eagle, over and around the families, watching what happens from a bird's-eye perspective (Figure 2.7). This can be done by literally leaving the circle of families, orbiting around them like a satellite, or leaving the room and watching via a video-link.

From this outside perspective it is possible to spot problematic intra- or inter-family interactions and to pick these out (Figure 2.8). The therapist can decide to move in and highlight a particular issue or interaction, addressing just the people concerned, or widening this to involve the whole group and ask for their responses and reflections.

Having worked briefly with a specific issue, the therapist can then again return to the 'circling' observer position – until he next spots another opportunity for intervention. This continuous positioning and repositioning implies ongoing perspective changes and illustrates to the families that multi-positional stances help to view things and act differently.

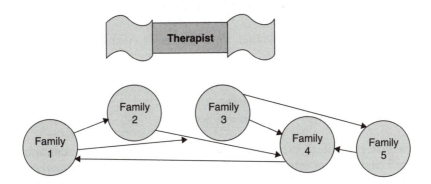

Therapist in bird perspective, seemingly calm but ready to 'pounce'.

Figure 2.7 Circling.

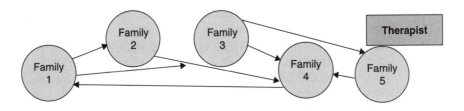

Therapist 'picks' a specific interaction and lets it resonate through MFT group.

Figure 2.8 Woodpecking.

The use of wider systemic interventions

MFT utilizes many techniques which have proved to be helpful in systemic couple or single family therapy, such as circular and reflexive questioning (Selvini Palazzoli *et al.* 1980; Tomm 1988), externalization (White and Epston 1990), boundary making and supporting personal autonomy (Minuchin 1974), and identifying and expanding resources (De Shazer 1982; Cooper-rider 1990). These techniques have been described in detail elsewhere and we shall therefore not elaborate on them further here. Other possibly less known techniques are also useful in MFT work and these will be outlined below.

Five-step model

The five-step model (Asen 1997) is a basic systemic intervention technique which can be employed in both single and multiple family therapy. It is a fitting tool when used in vivo during a session, with evolving intra- and inter-family interactions. There are five separate, though linked, steps that the therapist takes in order to focus an intervention in the here and now. These are:

1 Observing and 'punctuating' problematic interactions and communications.
2 Checking perceptions.
3 Inviting evaluation.
4 Determining the wish to change.
5 Encouraging experimentation and action.

As a *first step* the therapist voices what he believes to be an unusual or problematic intra- or inter-family interaction. It needs to be emphasized that what the therapist says is his construction, his punctuation, selected from a wide range of possible observations. Hopefully this punctuation is helpful and can serve to inform subsequent interventions. Here are a few examples of how this is done:

> 'I notice that . . .
> - you, Mum, want Craig to put his shoes on, but that he does not do this.
> - you, John, have decided to do exactly the opposite of what your mum is telling you.
> - you, Mr and Mrs Jones, want to talk to each other, but Paul continually interrupts you.
> - whenever Mrs Smith begins to say something, Mr Smith intervenes and completes the sentence.
> - your son seems to like Johnny's father a lot. He hardly knows him but sits on his lap and cuddles up to him.'

The *second step* consists of the therapist checking his observation with others, not only with members of one specific family but potentially also with the whole group: 'Do you also see it that way – or am I totally off the mark?' Since a therapist can never know in advance whether his observations are also shared by others, he needs to check this. If this is not the case and family members do not know what the therapist is talking about, then it is best not to insist on the alleged accuracy, or otherwise, of his observations but to retract these: 'I probably got that wrong.'

However, if the family agrees with the observational statement, it is time for the *third step*, namely to invite evaluation from the concerned family, its individual members or indeed the larger group: 'Are you happy that it is this way, or do you mind?' This question is meant to be open-ended and allows each person to reply with 'yes' or 'no' and should then lead them to explain how they arrived at their respective positions. The therapist can explore in detail why specific answers have been given and how they connect up, if at all. Mostly the response will be that other people share the observations and this allows moving to steps four and five. However, if the general answer is a wholehearted 'no' and the therapist still insists on pursuing his line of inquiry, then he is likely to meet a lot of resistance. For example, if parents say that they do not mind that their child continues to scream, the therapist can observe: 'You say that you don't mind that Johnny continues to scream – what might be the advantages and disadvantages of that? What do other families here think?' At times this helps families to identify what is appropriate and what is not – and what the implications of challenging a child or parent are. The aim is always for therapist and families to work together, and if a family or some of its members do not agree with the observations of the therapist, the latter needs to accept this. Therapists do well not to get caught up in a symmetrical escalation, but to stimulate reflective thinking instead. 'You say that you do not mind if Johnny continues screaming – and from what you tell us, he screams day and night at home and in the nursery. What do you think are the advantages and disadvantages if he continues to scream here for another few hours? What would happen in the nursery? What might be the consequences? What do other families here think?' In this way family members are encouraged to consider the pros and cons of action or inaction.

The *fourth step* invites family members to give voice to their views about change: 'So, if you do not want things to continue in this way, how would you like it to be?' In the above example, parents may reply: 'Well, that's obvious, we want him to stop screaming!' The therapist follows this up by taking the *fifth step*, to get family members to identify how to go about achieving this change: 'What would you have to say or do now to make it be the way you want it to be? What would be the first step?' Not infrequently families respond to this with some hesitation, inviting the therapist to provide the answers. He can then continue: 'What is stopping you from doing what you think you should be doing? What is the first little thing you might need to do?

Who else here has some ideas?' This last question aims to draw in the expertise of other families.

This seemingly concrete and simple format for framing and intervening helps therapists to pinpoint and address emerging interactions in the here and now. Often families behave as if they have no ideas about what to do differently and they almost inevitably turn to the therapist(s) for guidance and advice. They see therapists as 'experts' and themselves as 'helpless'. However, systemic therapists avoid getting hooked into such conscious or non-conscious interactions with their clients. Instead of merely answering questions put to them by families in a straightforward manner, therapists can divert the action by referring to the expertise of other families and their resources, for example by asking circular questions:

> 'Mrs W, what do you think about the question Mr J asked? How would you answer this? Who here would like to say something about the issues raised by Mrs W? Are these issues that might also be familiar to others in the room here? What would you say about what you observed going on between Jackie and her parents? I noticed that Jack always blames his parents – which of the other families here have noticed this? If you were to find yourselves in a situation like this, what might you want to do? Mrs J, could you during the next 30 minutes pretend that you are Mrs G and treat Tracy just the way her mother treats her? And you, Mrs G, just watch what happens. . . . What do the others here think about that?'

These and similar questions, asked in a group context, aim to involve all members of the group and invite them to offer their own perspectives and ideas.

The metaphor of a Greek chorus may be a fitting description of this process: its members offer comments on the developing (family) drama and the 'actors' can benefit from this feedback. It is also possible to dramatize this playfully by getting the chorus, in ritualized ways, to sing specific lines (Schweitzer-Rothers 2006). For example, certain internal monologues or dominant narratives of a parent, such as 'I can't manage that', 'Nobody values me' or 'He never ever listens to me' can be put to music, with the chorus of families singing this unhelpful mantra louder and louder, with emerging rhythmic and tonal variations and many repeats. A counter-refrain with new wordings, such as 'I can do it', can then be encouraged to emerge, accompanied by new rhythms and melodies. The therapist may initially be the 'conductor' and 'composer' of the chorus, but will soon encourage others to take over the (invisible) conducting baton and to experiment with amplifying new lines. This exercise is usually good fun and releases much energy and creativity, with the result of subduing the dominant narratives, at least for a time. The dramatization of inner voices or of the 'familiar broadcast' in a group context permits the development of alternative programmes and new tunes. With the help of other families, a new 'hit' can then be scripted.

Reflecting team techniques

A considerable number of techniques and practices used in MFT are derived from 'reflecting team' (Andersen 1987) techniques. These are based on the principle that an outside observing team sees and experiences things differently from those who are directly involved in the therapeutic process. In MFT it is not only therapists who have the potential for being a reflecting team, but also the other families and their members. The goldfish bowl technique uses an inner and an outer circle. For example, teenagers ('goldfish') can discuss a specific theme in an inner circle, with the parents ('cats') listening and observing this discussion. After some time there is a switchover, with the parents then sitting in the inner circle, reflecting on the discussion they had listened to and with the teenagers now assuming the outer circle listening position. At a later stage the young people can return to the insider position, reflecting on the reflections of their parents about their discussion. It is also possible, for example, to get mothers to discuss a particular issue and for the fathers to be in an observing position and then to switch over. The goldfish bowl technique not only furthers inter-family interactions and makes people aware of the frequent circularity of interactions, but also helps to emphasize the difference between 'thinking' and 'doing'.

Another useful technique derived from the reflecting team concept is 'flashlight'. This is a dedicated time slot during which action is temporarily suspended and time for reflection created. This implies a rapid context shift, from the heat of action to the relative coolness of reflection. The therapist may say: 'It's getting pretty hot here – a lot of noise, a lot of conflict. I think we should have a brief pause right away, to sit down and think about what's been happening just now.' Flashlight is a form of 'taking the temperature' not only of the whole group but also of its individual members. All other actions are frozen for a short while so as to create a reflective space. There are other related ways in which the healing powers of a group can work, such as using 'outsider witness group' (White 1997) rituals. Here different group members provide their own personal responses and resonances as a form of feedback to a specific family dilemma or charged situation.

We have already emphasized the need for MFT therapists to be active, flexible and multipositional and to be able to negotiate many context shifts within short spaces of time. This stance is transparent and visible to families and it can become 'catching': families themselves begin to become curious about other families and their dilemmas; they get better at making context shifts; they become increasingly more responsible for taking the initiative and experimenting with new interactions and behaviours. They learn that whilst therapists can provide some help, therapy can also happen when the therapist is not present. In situations where therapists, keeping in mind the group process, temporarily leave the therapy setting, families have to self-manage and become responsible for their own 'treatment'. However, this does not happen overnight as many families have considerable experience and skills to 'rope in' therapists and to get them involved in entrenched interactions. This can lead to therapeutic paralysis, with therapists no longer being able to think and act spontaneously and creatively. The knowledge that, as a therapist, one is still mobile, physically and mentally, can be aided by taking on different spatial positions in the therapy room – or outside it. Being able to move physically, to stand up and to 'get out' of it, may at times be necessary and can feel liberating, helping to develop new perspectives. If therapists do fully believe that all families have greater or lesser degrees of self-healing potential, then taking a backseat, or even absenting oneself temporarily, is a way of signalling to families to take charge themselves. Together with other families they can take on responsibility and use their own resources to make 'their' therapeutic context more meaningful.

Further techniques

Video feedback

Video feedback is used to great effect in MFT. To see oneself from a different angle can help to pinpoint strengths and difficulties. In conversation with other families in a reflective setting, new perspectives and ideas for change emerge. Audiovisual recordings of problematic situations and interactions can be viewed and analysed in a group setting. Such recordings can be made on site or families can be encouraged to take video (DVD) cameras home, so that they can film situations they regard as 'good' or 'bad'. No matter who the cameraman (or woman) is – father, mother, adolescent or granny – such home movies are useful accounts of family life and troubles. When screened in the presence of an audience of families who struggle with similar issues, this can become a powerful tool for change. In MFT day settings, regular video feedback sessions tend to be built into the programme and can take place daily, either on an impromptu basis when a specific interaction has occurred that warrants immediate re-viewing, or else at set times. The group of families, experts in their own right, are encouraged to reflect on what they see, to ask questions and to make suggestions.

Role reversals

Role reversals have much therapeutic potential as the participants assume an unfamiliar role within their family. For example, children can be asked to act, for a limited time, as if they were their own parents – while the parents role play their children: 'For the next ten minutes, can each parent role play their child and each child their mother or father. Dear parents, in the role of your child you can be as well or badly behaved as you like – and you, dear children, as your own mum or dad, try to take control over your children and try to manage them.' The ensuing mayhem is not only fun for all concerned but also highly informative. Parents often report how surprised they were to hear their children, when role playing their parents, using identical words to those they use, making it difficult for them to claim subsequently that my child never listens to me. Children can also assume the therapist's role and this can be more playful and creative if they are supplied with the necessary props, such as a white coat and stethoscope: 'We want *you* to be the experts, therapists, doctors or psychologists, and we want you to decide what should happen next, who should be examined and what treatment to give to whom.'

Cross-fostering

Cross-fostering is a technique used to promote new experiences and related perspective changes. Here a child is 'fostered' with another family attending MFT for one hour or longer. In return, the 'foster' family's own child is temporarily placed with the parent(s) of the first family. A task or exercise is given to each family and in a subsequent 'flashlight' the families discuss their experiences and attempt to answer questions such as why it is more difficult to manage one's own child than the child of another family. Children can be asked to talk about why they think that the 'foster' parents were more sensitive to their requests. When managing the children of other families, many parents discover hidden or long-forgotten competencies which they can use later with their own children.

Yellow and red cards

Yellow and red cards are issued to families so that, as a kind of shorthand, they can signal and flag up specific issues. For example, if specific interactions have been agreed by the group as being problematic – like swearing, or talking too long, or a child being disruptive – group members can raise a yellow card as a first warning and a red card the second time round. The consequences of being shown a red card are then discussed between families, as well as whether the 'foul' deserved such severe punishment. Green cards can be held up when a family or an individual group member is performing well.

Certificates

Certificates, prints of digital photographs taken during MFT work, documents such as a 'Parental Driving Licence', can be issued as living proof of achievements made during the course of therapeutic work. These have a different meaning in a group context than they would have in single family work as they are a public acknowledgement of success. Celebration of success is important for many families and certificates or other documents can be taken home and displayed prominently.

Typical difficulties and problem situations

In this section we describe commonly encountered problem scenarios that can arise in the course of MFT. We provide some pragmatic suggestions so as to assist therapists.

A parent does not participate in MFT

Work reasons → Meet with absent person (frequently the father) and family jointly (possibly during a home visit after working hours). The possibility of shift work or taking annual leave to attend MFT can be discussed. In the MFT group, other parents are asked which strategies they have used successfully to get a seemingly reluctant parent to attend. If a father attends one meeting as a 'trial', one can emphasize the importance of this: 'I am very happy that you have managed to come here today, despite your huge work commitments. We all hope that you will be able to see at the end of the day how important your presence has been for your child and partner – and maybe even for yourself.'

Lack of interest and/or poor engagement → Group members become 'advocates' for the importance of parental presence. The group collects arguments as to why the reluctant parent should attend. These can be rehearsed, via a role play, so that the mother can use them later at home. Members of the group can also undertake a home visit to motivate the reluctant parent.

A child plays up and does not do what the parents want him to do, with formation of unhelpful coalitions and/or splitting of the parental alliance by child

→ Get detailed description – or video example – of typical issue and reflect in group about alternative solutions. Possibly stage 'play' with old and new 'scripts', played by 'actors' recruited from other families, with concerned family then watching this (their) 'play'.

Scapegoating and marginalization

Person in 'victim' position → Address whole group: 'Who here has been in a position of being a scapegoat? What is it like when you are being scapegoated – how do you feel, what do you think? Is it possible to get out of that position all by yourself? What help can one expect to get?' A role play can follow, with volunteers placing themselves in victim position and experimenting with alternative behaviours: 'What would need to happen for you to get out of that position? Who do you need to talk to? What do you want to say? What should you not say? What can others do about it – and what can you do yourself? What's the first step you can take?'

Family in 'outsider' position → Play inclusion games (see later chapters).

Family member leaves room or setting

Child leaves room as she or he feels unnoticed → Make parent responsible for recovering the child: 'Mr P, have you noticed that Mary is no longer in this room? Is that okay with you? Do you know where she is and whether she is safe? Whose job do you think it is to find her? What do other families think?'

Child leaves room in order to avoid parental challenges (and parents behave as if they were paralysed or they feel very ashamed) → Ask parent: 'Do you think that your child needs you now? What would happen if you were to go after your child now and therefore showed her that it is *you* who has the say here? Who of the other families thinks that Mr G should be in charge – who thinks that he should just give up?'

Parent leaves room (lack of interest or *'It's all too much'*) → Ask other member of family group, preferably one who has formed some relationship with that parent, to convince him or her to return.

Parent feels helpless and useless

→ Search for successful strategies the parent may have used in past, or in other social situations, or by other members of the extended family. Other families are invited to bring in their own experiences of success.

Parent minimizes problems

→ Ask parent(s): 'Have I got this right, in that you do not see your child's difficulties as being that serious? Do you think that if you do nothing, things will get better or worse? Who of the other parents here agrees – who has a different opinion?'

Rivalries and aggression between families

→ Actively stop or disrupt the actual confrontation and perhaps suggest a 'flashlight' or 'freezing' of the action.

Starting the work

We have already explained that MFT can be carried out in closed or open groups. In a closed group all families start and end therapy at the same time. The work can begin with an initial 'tasting' event which should give families a flavour of what there is to come and to get them to make informed decisions as to whether this is something they wish to commit themselves to. Multi-family tasting events, which last one to two hours, are best scheduled in the late afternoon or early evening so that sceptical participants find it more difficult to cite work commitments as a reason for non-attendance. It is important that the meeting is well structured, given that between 20 to 40 people may turn up and the potential for ensuing chaos is therefore considerable. Many families will, of course, be apprehensive about attending a meeting with people who are not known to them. In order to avoid creating unnecessary anxieties in the families, therapists need to take the lead. The meeting room and environment need to be welcoming, including providing refreshments. This allows families, as they enter, to get hold of something and to meet informally over a glass of juice and some finger food. The therapists will try to assist families in making first steps to get to know other people in the room, which is set up with chairs in rows which face a podium or stage, like in a lecture theatre. This is in line with a major idea prevailing in the field of systemic therapies: the therapist is responsible for making a good context which allows families to feel safe and at ease to explore and address specific issues. The therapist is *not* responsible for the families or children in the room, signalling that this is the job of the responsible adults.

After this somewhat formal introduction it is the therapists' task to facilitate the encounter between families and to enable them to exchange ideas and experiences. This can be done by moving chairs and forming a big circle: 'Can you please all help so that we can form a big circle, so that we can see and face each other, without straining our necks and backs too much.' Once the circle is formed, a number of exercises can be used to help families to get to know each other (see Chapter 3).

Introductory MFT tastings can be helpful in reducing families' anxieties about attending a group. If ex-service users are invited – families that have already participated in MFT – then their experiences can be an inspiration for newcomers. However, tastings are not always necessary, particularly if the groups are 'open'. Here we already have a stable core of families who have worked together for a while and there is usually good group cohesion. When a new family arrives, it can be connected with an 'old' one.

> *Therapist:* 'Mr and Mrs A, you have been coming here for a little while. Maybe you can explain to this new family, the Bs, what it has been like for you to come here. Perhaps you can talk about what happens, what you think and feel about working with other families and what you have got out of coming here. And do not forget to tell them what you found difficult.'

Chapter 3

Setting the scene

MFT group exercises

MFT exercises and playful activities

In this chapter we describe exercises and playful activities which aim to make the multi-family group a safe and creative context for all participants – young and old. Given that at the outset of MFT work families usually do not know each other, they will be apprehensive, if not anxious, about talking about themselves and their specific problems in front of strangers. Playful exercises and activities can break the ice, as well as enabling families to explore and address specific issues and themes. Furthermore, joint exercises help to build group cohesion and team spirit, and get group members to develop a healthy interest in others. The exercises described in this chapter can be used not only at the beginning but also during other phases of MFT, as well as in single family therapy contexts. Some exercises have also been described elsewhere and others have been adapted from ideas suggested by colleagues (Asen and Tomson 1992; Asen *et al.* 2001, 2004; Retzlaff 2008; Schemmel *et al.* 2008).

We have subdivided the exercises into three categories and labelled them accordingly for ease of use. In this chapter we primarily describe those exercises and playful activities which relate to group issues (therefore marked with **G**), but they are also meant to have specific meaning for each family and their individual members. Exercises and activities that more specifically address intra-family issues are marked with **F** and are described in Chapter 4. Chapter 5 covers exercises which focus on specific problems and presentations (**P**). We are well aware that the division into three categories is somewhat arbitrary, but nevertheless think that it may be a useful map for general orientation and action.

There are different ways in which the exercises and playful activities can be used. It is possible to do them with all families together, as a kind of group exercise involving everybody. Other exercises can be undertaken by each family on their own first and their experiences can then be shared with the group afterwards. For example, when each family is asked to do their own 'Life River' (F9), they present their completed task to the rest of the families, with the therapist facilitating this. The focus is therefore on one particular family first, with the other families listening and then asking questions, as well as reflecting on what has been said and on the implications for themselves. They can be asked to resonate with the experiences of other families and then consider how they might tackle similar issues in their own families. Once the work with one family is completed, the therapist can move on to the next. Whilst this may seem a fair way of doing things, it can carry a risk of becoming repetitive and monotonous. On the whole we have found it useful to work with two families in the large group context first, but then to get the remaining families to pair up with one another and to interview each other about the exercise and the different contributions each family member may have made. This is an easier task for families once they have observed how the therapist has done this with two families. The therapist can introduce this process by saying: 'You have observed how we therapists talked about the exercise with family X and family Z. Now we could do the same with the four remaining families, but we suggest that you take over and that you each find one other family with whom you can discuss the matter. The Xs and Zs can join each family pair and assist them.' This enables the therapists to begin 'circling' (around the families) and let the families work amongst themselves: 'Do this for the next 20 minutes (ten minutes for each family) and then the Xs and Zs can later tell us what they observed.'

What should the time frame of the exercises be? There is no single or simple answer to this question as it very much depends on the work context and the nature of the exercise. As a general rule 10 to 30 minutes for each family to carry out the exercise or playful activity seems appropriate. The subsequent presentations and discussions can last between 60 and 90 minutes.

In order to help readers and clinicians with the use of these exercises and playful activities, we have described each under a number of headings. We make suggestions as to their *use* – namely under what circumstances therapists may wish to employ them. However, we do hope that readers will discover their own context-specific uses. The *sequence* of each exercise is outlined and the therapeutic *aims* are defined. We list the necessary *materials* and provide the *instructions* in direct speech, so as to help therapists with the pragmatics of making it work. The *work focus* contains specific suggestions for the direction of therapeutic work and *critical situations* which may occur are mentioned, with → *tips* as to how to manage them. The exercises can be carried out in a number of different ways: individually by each person, with everyone doing it on their own; children and parents can complete the exercises in parallel or together; and sometimes one or two families may do so, with the other families observing and reflecting. No matter how the exercise is started, it is almost always important that at some stage all families discuss their impressions or discoveries in the multi-family context, so that an exchange between families can take place. It is possible to use terms other than 'exercises' and sometimes families, particularly with young children, prefer the term 'games' or 'activities'.

A major aim of many of the exercises described in this chapter is to help the group of families to coalesce and to become a kind of 'team'. We start with ice breakers and then proceed to exercises that address issues such as trust, playfulness and roles. The goal is to make the group a safe and creative context and to enable all participants to experiment with new ideas and actions, overcoming their anxieties and inhibitions.

G1 CONNECTING FAMILIES

USE
First MFT meetings, tasting evening, or when new families join.

SEQUENCE
All members of the families sit in a circle. A ball is thrown from person to person. The ball catcher answers specific questions and responds to tasks.

AIMS
To facilitate mutual introductions and for the group members to get to know each other. To find out about similarities and differences. To promote mutual 'curiosity'.

MATERIALS
Soft ball.

INSTRUCTION
'This ball is going to be thrown from one person to another. Whoever catches it, should say their name.'

Next round: 'Whoever catches the ball, should say one of their likes and one dislike' (e.g. food, hobby, music, etc.).

Next round: 'Whoever catches the ball should say two sentences about a member of their family.'

Later: 'Whoever catches the ball should try and remember what the person who threw the ball said about themselves and their family.'

WORK FOCUS
Who can relate to what? What is familiar – what is different? What do families and their individual members have in common?

CRITICAL SITUATIONS
One group member refuses to participate → therapist accepts this, rather than confronting the issue.

G2 SPEED DATING

USE
Initial stages of MFT, as well as during later phases when focusing on specific issues, as a tool for reflecting quickly about a specific issue.

SEQUENCE
An inner circle of family members is interviewed by an outer circle around a specific question/issue – and this is then reversed. Initially two minutes for each person is allowed, but this is subsequently reduced to much shorter timespans (60, 30 and 15 seconds), with members of the outer circle moving at the therapist's signal clockwise, sitting opposite new members. The speed is increased and the group gets energized.

AIMS
To act as an 'ice breaker' and to help group members to get to know each other. To talk and reflect quickly about a specific issue.

MATERIALS
Inner and outer circles of chairs.

INSTRUCTION
'Can we have all seven children, please . . . and can you sit here in the middle, forming a circle that looks outwards. And can we have the adults forming an outside circle but looking inwards, so that an adult is placed opposite a child. Can you interview each other about your likes and dislikes. You have only two minutes each to find this out and when we ring the bell, the adults have to move one seat to the left – and then you do the same thing again. And later it will get faster and faster – you'll get quite breathless.'

Variation: other issues that can be discussed include what happened in school yesterday or at home last night; the problem that has brought people to the group? One wish that they would want to come true?

WORK FOCUS
What has each person found out about someone else? What are the most popular hobbies? What did you find about the problems people have? What do you have in common?

CRITICAL SITUATIONS
Participants cannot find words to get started → therapist kneels next to them and feeds questions to each and then disengages.

G3 FINDING YOUR PLACE

USE

Families from different cultures and backgrounds, initial stages of MFT.

SEQUENCE

A variety of tasks is given to highlight visually differences and future actions.

AIMS

To mark where families come from and where they might wish to move/ migrate to.

MATERIALS

Large space to move around in.

INSTRUCTION

'If you look around and at each other you can see that we all look quite different. Some are tall and others are shorter. Why don't you form a line, defined by height. This means that the tallest person should be on the left end of the line and the smallest on the right end. Just line yourselves up and each person should place themselves where they think they fit.'

Next round: 'This time we want people to place themselves according to the colour of their hair: those with very black hair on the very left and those with white blonde hair on the very right – and the rest should find their places somewhere between those poles.'

Next round: 'Now we want people to place themselves according to where members of your families come from. This won't be easy if they come from very different parts of the world – you need to decide which ones you choose. We will make a few spaces: right in the middle we want people whose families come from this place (e.g. London) and if you come from not so far away, place yourself near the centre. If you come from another country we will find some space – like Europe, Asia, America, Africa and Australia/New Zealand. Now place yourselves.'

Next round: 'Now imagine we live in the future, maybe in ten years time. You can move or migrate to wherever you want. Please go there and place yourself in the country and continent where you want to be.'

WORK FOCUS

How easy is it to find your place? What happens when members of the same family move to different spaces and get separated? How do you decide what your most important or most significant roots are? How do you plan together what to do in the future? How is difference and cultural diversity managed?

CRITICAL SITUATIONS

Difficulties of knowing where to place oneself if there are many different cultural roots → experiment with different places and how each feels.

G4 MAGIC FOREST

USE

Families with pre-adolescent children.

SEQUENCE

Families are asked to set up an imaginary forest and to change into playful animal families.

AIMS

To experiment with closeness and care in a playful context. To increase intra- and inter-family cohesion.

MATERIALS

Pot plants, branches, leaves, paper trees, blankets.

INSTRUCTION

'Imagine that you are all animals and that you all live peacefully together in a magic forest. What sort of animals might you want to be? Deer, elephants, moles, mice, birds, snakes, lions? Can each family decide for themselves what kind of animal family you want to be – or what you are going to do if each family member wants to be a different animal. Please build a nest or other kind of home on this magic mountain.'

Variation: 'Now there is a forest fire. How can the animal families help each other?'

WORK FOCUS

How did you feel as animal families? What was different from how things are usually? How did you get on with the other animals and their families? What happened when the forest fire broke out? What of this is relevant for your own home now?

CRITICAL SITUATIONS

Difficulties with closeness and regression → ad hoc brief conversations so as to talk about resonances from the past ('What did this trigger in you – what are you feeling and thinking when you do this?')

G5 GROUP ANIMAL

USE

Families with diversity of cultural and ethnic origins.

SEQUENCE

All families collaborate with creating a huge picture which symbolizes the strengths of the group.

AIMS

To increase group cohesion.

MATERIALS

Huge paper canvas, colouring pencils.

> **INSTRUCTION**
> 'We would like to ask you all to make a picture of this group, one picture made by all of you together – but in the form of a mythical animal, which shows above all the strengths of this group. It would be best if you can first agree on what this animal might look like and then who starts with what bit. For example, you might want to start with the feet – and you with the tail and maybe you with the head.'

WORK FOCUS

What are the strengths of this group? How did you come to an agreement? What could you not agree on? What would one have to do for the animal to get even stronger?

CRITICAL SITUATIONS

Indecision or disagreements → divide group and paint/draw a second animal. Then compare animals and encourage families to decide to make a combined animal, taking bits from each.

G6 KINGDOM

USE

Poorly structured families, or families with rigidly defined roles.

SEQUENCE

Families create a kingdom in which each finds their role.

AIMS

To achieve transparency in relation to how roles get chosen/allocated. To work with hierarchies. To encourage a change of roles.

MATERIALS

Papier mâché, hats, crowns, status symbols.

INSTRUCTION

'Imagine you live in a kingdom, far, far away. Please decide who lives in your kingdom – like king, queen, prince, princess, maid, servant, fool, knight, peasant, craftsman, merchant, jailer, etc. Once you have decided who is who, please find ways of dressing up – you can make hats, crowns, jewellery, tools – whatever you like. Then make a kingdom where everything works out well.'

Variation: 'Let's imagine there is a revolution against royalty!'

WORK FOCUS

Is everyone satisfied with their role? Who would like to change it? How can you negotiate this – and with whom?

CRITICAL SITUATIONS

Rebellion against the 'all powerful' → let it be played out and get families to consider restoring 'law and order'.

G7 FAIRY TALE WORLD

USE

Families with pre-adolescent children.

SEQUENCE

Making of masks, or use of dresses, development of story/tale, which includes all participants. Staging/performance and recording on video, subsequent viewing with all families and discussion.

AIMS

To make visible the visions and dreams of each family member and its use as resources for therapy. To encourage families to work together.

MATERIALS

Version 1: fancy dress(es).

Version 2: paper, colouring pencils, possibly facepaint, glue, scissors, decorations.

INSTRUCTION

'What type of person/character would you love to play? Create a costume and/or mask which represents this figure. Then introduce yourself briefly to the group in this new role. The group then has 45 minutes to invent a story or tale in which all the roles have a place. We will then produce the play. How can you be a princess for a day at home?'

WORK FOCUS

Who has taken which role for what purpose? How did people experience developing a common story? What went really well, what did not? Who takes responsibility for what, such as sticking to time frames? Who is 'in charge', what work structures evolve?

CRITICAL SITUATIONS

Some adults do not want to play → involve them in filming the event.

G8 ROBINSON CRUSOE'S ISLAND

USE

Middle and end phases of MFT.

SEQUENCE

Families are all on a cruise on an ocean liner. Ship runs on to rocks and sinks, families arrive at lonely island and need to survive.

AIMS

To experiment with intra- and inter-family roles and crisis management.

MATERIALS

Improvised lifeboat, improvised island with jungle and without people.

INSTRUCTION

'Imagine you are all on a cruise on this wonderful ocean liner. All is comfortable, you are enjoying life, there are no worries. But suddenly the boat hits a rock and the boat sinks – everyone has to jump ship and use the lifeboat which cannot take everybody – what are you going to do? And when you arrive on the island there is nobody there. The captain and ship personnel remain on board the sinking vessel, so the families have to help themselves. What do you do when you arrive on the island, how are you going to survive? Please find ways of making a script together and play these situations.'

WORK FOCUS

How did each family organize itself? How did the families work together? How were roles allocated? How can one create structure in chaotic situations?

CRITICAL SITUATIONS

Chaos ensues → Flashlight: 'What is going to happen if you continue like this? How many of you would drown or starve?'

G9 SURPRISE BIRTHDAY PARTY

USE
'Chaotic' families.

SEQUENCE
Families are asked to throw a surprise birthday party for one child. They first plan and then give it. Individual family members subsequently reflect about their last birthday.

AIMS
To generate creativity and foster spontaneity and experimentation. To practise improvisational skills. To work together as a team with role allocation.

MATERIALS
Fancy dress, 'presents' and other birthday props.

INSTRUCTION
'Imagine you have just found out that it is X's birthday today (pointing at one child). You are all here and want to give X a birthday party. How do you go about it? Please plan a party during the next 15 minutes – and then give it. X, you are not allowed to hear anything about it, so you have to sit/play with us for that time in another room.'

WORK FOCUS
Who plans what? What is the role of the actual parent(s)? How do families work together? How important are presents?

CRITICAL SITUATIONS
Actual parent very rejecting of child → get 'adoptive' parent to role play.

G10 BLINDFOLD

USE
Early phase of MFT.

SEQUENCE
Children blindfold their parents and ask them to find them in a big room – with children giving clues. This is then reversed and the children look for their parents. 'Blind' parents can be led by children through a 'minefield'. Roles can then be reversed. Subsequent cross-family linkage.

AIMS
To explore issues to do with trust and 'blind' faith.

MATERIALS
Blindfolds.

> **INSTRUCTION**
> 'We want to play a game – it's about trust and who we can trust when and where. We have got a few blindfolds here and we want the parents to be blindfolded – so that they can really not see anything. And then we want their children to lead them through this room and perhaps even outside. Later we are going to make a pretend minefield and the children will have to be really careful to lead their parents through it. Then we want to turn the tables and the children are blindfolded and the parents lead them.'

WORK FOCUS
What was it like to be blind? Did you feel in good hands? When can you trust whom – and when not? Would you have found it easier to be led by someone from another family? Why don't you try it out?

CRITICAL SITUATIONS
Panic by blindfolded person → therapist interviews person to find out what their worst fears are.

G11 LABELS

USE
All phases of MFT.

SEQUENCE
Each person in each family is given a sticker and is asked to write specific descriptions on it. People then walk around and look at each other's stickers and ask questions.

AIMS
To get to know each other and find out about specific issues. During later stages of MFT to address issues of feeling unfairly 'labelled' by others.

MATERIALS
Stickers, pens, scissors.

INSTRUCTION
'People here are new, they haven't met before. Could each of you write five words (or drawings) on this little sticker which say something about you as a person and stick it on. You can then walk around the room and look at what people have said about themselves – and ask questions if you like.'

Variation: 'Write down first impressions others have of you (correct or not) – what is it that you do that gives people the impression that you are . . .?'

Variation: 'Write your favourite animal – or an animal that represents you – on the label – and then talk to each other about why you might have chosen this – and how you may have similar traits to the animal.'

WORK FOCUS
What have you learned about each other? What was most/least surprising? What should there be more/less of? How accurate or fitting are labels? What labels have to be given – and what do you feel/think about this? What is it that you do that gives people the impression that you are . . .? How do you get rid of a label?

CRITICAL SITUATIONS
Participants cannot write (illiterate, young children) → mime (like on television show *Give Us a Clue!*)

G12 FROZEN STATUES

USE
All families.

SEQUENCE
Each participant represents a snapshot of a feeling state.

AIMS
To improve non-verbal understanding. To display and recognize the presentation and recognition of different feeling states (self and others).

MATERIALS
Flipchart, possibly digital camera.

INSTRUCTION
'Who here can name some feelings? Can you just name some and I will write them down on this flipchart. What does it look like when you are happy, sad, angry or aggressive? Show this and freeze the feeling state in your face and body? Look at each other so you can see how differently people show their feelings? [Each feeling is given two or three minutes.] So that's how different being sad can look.'

Variation: 'I will take a quick photo of each statue so that we can all look at this afterwards.'

WORK FOCUS
How can one express and recognize different feelings? Can they be read accurately? How can one know how others feel? How can one fake feelings? When did anyone last feel like this?

Variation: Joint viewing of photos and guessing of each person's feeling.

CRITICAL SITUATIONS
Strong emotional reactions → therapist calms emotions down, enlisting the help of family members.

G13 BODY FEELINGS

USE
Families with difficulties talking about feelings.

SEQUENCE

Draw body contours of each person and each person then draws in specific feelings and where they are located.

AIMS

To identify, locate and talk about good and bad feelings.

MATERIALS

Wallpaper roll, colouring pencils.

INSTRUCTION

This exercise is preceded by getting the group members to name typical feelings. These get written on a flipchart so that group members can refer to them when completing the exercise.

'All of us have plenty of feelings and emotions – even if we hide them from others or from ourselves. And often we know what we feel, but not always where we feel it. We would like you to make a body outline of each person here, and for everyone to take it in turns to lie down on this wallpaper roll. Then someone will draw the outline of your body. Each person will then get their picture and is requested to use different colours to draw in the feelings they have, put them wherever you think they "live" – in your head, tummy, legs or wherever.'

WORK FOCUS

What do you notice about where certain feelings are located in different individuals and families? What can you do if you don't like the feelings? How can you decrease bad feelings and enlarge good feelings? What sort of stories come to mind when you had these feelings?

CRITICAL SITUATIONS

One person gets overwhelmed by feelings and cries profusely → ask where these feelings 'live' in the body and enlist members of other families to talk about how they place and manage overwhelming feelings.

GI4 LIE DETECTOR

USE

Early stages of MFT.

SEQUENCE

Each person is asked to make two statements about themselves – one which is true and one which is a lie. Other participants are then asked to guess which statement is true and which not.

AIMS

To increase inter-family curiosity. To learn about each other. To tune into non-verbal and para-verbal communication.

MATERIALS

None required.

INSTRUCTION

'We have hardly met before and know very little about each other. When one meets new people, one doesn't usually say much about oneself and often not the truth. We therefore want to ask everyone to make two statements about themselves – one which is true and another which is a lie – without letting anyone know what is true and what is not. Try to act in such a way that it is not possible for anyone to work out what is true and what not.'

WORK FOCUS

Who has the best poker face? Who is the best liar? When is it not advisable to tell the truth about oneself? Should we always be truthful? Is keeping up a façade important or not?

CRITICAL SITUATIONS

One person ridicules game → do not challenge, but place him or her in the position of guessing what is true and what is not.

G15 FRICTION GENERATES WARMTH

USE

Families with teenagers and conflicts.

SEQUENCE

In two parallel groups (duration approximately 45 minutes) parents and teenagers discuss the theme 'Friction Creates Warmth' and relate this to inter-personal relationships. Each group then presents a summary of their discussion to the other group via a poster, role play or other means.

AIMS

To address boundaries and rules. To explore how dealing with difference has both positive and negative aspects and can generate different feelings. To discuss the difference between discussion and confrontation.

MATERIALS

Paper, video and other materials to present 'results'.

INSTRUCTION

'In physics there is this principle that friction generates warmth. Please transfer this on to human relationships and discuss how this principle might also be a useful way of thinking about family dynamics. Sometimes there is a lot of tension in families, between teenagers and their parents, and what goes on is anything but "cold". What can lead to warmth and how can one stop soon enough, before things hot up too much? Please discuss this in two separate groups in different rooms and we will then ask you to present the results to each other later – in any way you want to.'

WORK FOCUS

When are differences of opinion important? What are the ground rules for a good discussion? What are the positive aspects of conflicts? Can disagreements and control also be seen as the expression of love and care? Do healthy teenagers need friction in order to learn to manage conflicts and to make up afterwards?

CRITICAL SITUATIONS

Group members find it impossible to see that there could be any positive aspects of conflict or difference of opinions → ask participants to remember their teenage years and give examples of major confrontations and how these might have been important for personality development.

G16 CIRCLE GAME

USE

Open or semi-open MFT groups, when new members join.

SEQUENCE

All group members are asked to form a big circle, with people joining up and not leaving any spaces. Individual participants are asked to leave the circle and for the circle then to close up again, with people holding hands. One by one each person is asked to break back into the circle, with the group trying to make this impossible.

In a second version participants are asked to go into the centre of the circle and to break out, again with the group resisting.

AIMS

To deal with issues of marginalization. To improve group cohesion and self-confidence. To thematize inclusion and exclusion.

MATERIALS

None.

INSTRUCTION

'Please place yourselves in a big circle, with people joining hands and arms, not leaving a single gap. Look inside the circle. One of you, maybe you Peter, comes out of the circle and the circle closes up again. Peter, you need to find a way to get into this circle, right into the middle. Find a gap, or create one – try hard to get in there, any trick you want to use, but you must not hurt anybody.'

Variation: break out of circle (one person is 'trapped' inside the circle and has to get out).

WORK FOCUS

How is it possible to 'fit in' or enter a circle of friends? Is it possible to hold on to each other? Is it possible to remain an individual? Which tricks are permitted – and which are not (tickle, humour, words) in order to 'get in'? How important is it to belong?

CRITICAL SITUATIONS

Inappropriate use of physical force → 'flashlight': what is acceptable physical force and what is not? Inhibited participant(s) → support: 'Who here could help you to get into the circle – your father or another child?'

G17 TUG OF WAR

USE

Families with power struggles.

SEQUENCE

Two teams are formed and a member of one of the families is the referee (this could be, for example, a person with a physical disability). The membership of the teams is then varied.

AIMS

To help each other to relax and feel good. To explore the different strength each person has.

MATERIALS

Thick rope (10–12 m), large room, garden or park.

INSTRUCTION

'You worked really hard during the past few hours. The children are getting more and more restless. How about using up any surplus energy and converting it into action. How about playing tug of war? Let's form two teams – maybe first all the children on one side and the parents on the other. Who knows who is going to win? Later you can also mix the teams and pick a few children for the parents' team – and a few parents for the children's team. We also need a referee – who is going to volunteer? The referee can explain the rules and make sure people stick to them. And we will have a few rounds.'

WORK FOCUS

What is fun and when do things get serious – is there an overlap? Who is the strongest team and why? Should one let the weaker ones win? Are tricks allowed? Who felt close to whom during the game? What experiences do people have of working as teams?

CRITICAL SITUATIONS

Some members become very competitive and rough → referee is encouraged to let these members play act being 'weak' and keen to lose.

G18 HEALTH FARM

USE

Parents who feel burnt out or run down.

SEQUENCE

Half of the group members sit on chairs. Behind each person stands another one, the 'feel good worker'. It is their task to make the sitting person, the client, feel good. This can be done via massage, words, or anything else that furthers relaxation. This has to be done in a way that is acceptable to the 'client'. The workers move every three minutes to the next client, clockwise. On another day the workers become clients and vice versa.

MATERIALS

Chairs placed in circle for half the members of group. Soothing music. Candles.

AIMS

To build trust. To help each other to relax and feel good and to find out what is acceptable for whom. To practise empathy.

INSTRUCTION

'You have all worked very hard today – wouldn't it be good to take a rest and be pampered? Have you ever been to a health farm? We certainly haven't – much too expensive and time consuming! The good news is that we have a health farm here. All we need is a bit of imagination. Let's imagine that half of you are clients and the other half are staff. We'll give everyone a number, 1 and 2. All the 1s are staff and all the 2s are clients. The clients have to arrange their chairs in a circle facing inwards – and the staff take their position behind the client – one person behind each chair. You are the "feel good worker". For three minutes it is your job to make you client relax and recover their energy. You can use your hands and massage – but only if your client allows you to. Or you can talk or even sing to them to make them feel good. You might use music or whatever. But it is important that your client likes what you do – otherwise they can't feel good. After three minutes you move on to the next client.'

WORK FOCUS

How easy and how difficult is it to relax? Have you noticed differences in how you have been treated? Do you have a 'feel good worker' in your family? How can you train them up? What did you not like? Were you able to tell the worker? How did your 'client' respond?

CRITICAL SITUATIONS

One 'worker' is too insensitive to 'client's' needs and unable to take feedback → therapist pauses and convenes team of other 'workers' for consultation.

G19 OUTINGS

USE
Disorganized families.

SEQUENCE
The families plan an outing (zoo, shopping centre, market, museum).

AIMS
To increase group cohesion. To amplify parental competences.

MATERIALS
Tickets, picnic.

INSTRUCTION
'We would like to do an outing with all of you next week. Let's talk about where we might go and what we might do. Each family is responsible for the outing and their child(ren), their care and safety. Do bring enough money/food and make sure there is appropriate clothing.'

WORK FOCUS
What are/were the difficult situations? How did the different families manage these? How did the families get on with each other? How did you manage disagreements?

CRITICAL SITUATIONS
Children find themselves in risk situations (traffic, strangers) → parents are immediately asked to consider risks and how to reduce them.

G20 FINISHING

USE
End of MFT.

SEQUENCE
The responsibility for structuring the last day of an MFT group is given to the group and they are warned about this during the penultimate meeting. All the planning is left to the group and its members.

AIMS

To help families to understand that they themselves can create meaningful contexts for addressing specific issues.

MATERIALS

Group members bring their own materials or use existing ones.

INSTRUCTION

None.

WORK FOCUS

What do you make of it all?

CRITICAL SITUATIONS

Families behave passively → therapists behave even more passively.

G21 GOODBYE RITUALS

USE

End of MFT (closed group). When one family leaves (open group).

SEQUENCE

Preparation prior to this MFT session, with group members being encouraged to consider devising goodbye rituals.

AIMS

To get families to take responsibility for completing a 'course' of MFT.

MATERIALS

Group members bring/make their own materials.

INSTRUCTION

'Next time we meet it is the last time for the group (or for family B). How might you want to mark this? What would you all want to happen? Should there be a formal ceremony – with speeches, certificates or should it just be an informal celebration? Can you all think about this and we leave it to you to organize the day.'

WORK FOCUS

What are the advantages and disadvantages about celebrating an ending? Who should issue certificates?

CRITICAL SITUATIONS

Families 'forget' → therapist asks them to improvise then and there.

Chapter 4

Family-oriented exercises

The exercises presented in this chapter address above all intra-family issues and relationship problems. They aim to make overt hidden thoughts, feelings and values. Families need to know other families a little bit before embarking on some of these exercises as they may feel forced to talk about issues that are too personal. Many of the exercises can also be applied to single family work. However, in a multi-family setting the responses and reflections of other families, provide an additional powerful context within which specific family and individual issues can be explored.

F1 COAT OF ARMS

USE
Disorganized families.

SEQUENCE
Each family designs its own coat of arms which describes strengths and specific characteristics. This is presented to the large group and discussed.

AIMS
To increase family cohesion via defining and strengthening the family's identity.

MATERIALS
White cardboard, colouring pencils and paint.

INSTRUCTION
'In the good old days, families – certainly the noble ones – had their own coats of arms that said something about their past history, their motto and their strengths. A lot of pride was invested in the coat of

arms. We would like to invite each family to design such a coat of arms for itself. As a family think about what is special about your family, what you are proud of and what specific strengths you have. Transform all this into a coat of arms, and if you can then think of a family motto, so much the better.'

WORK FOCUS

What are the family strengths? How can important past family history be contained in the coat of arms? What are the positives about each family? What might be the family motto? What should the coat of arms look like in the future?

CRITICAL SITUATIONS

Poverty of ideas or negative attitude → other members of group are invited to comment on the perceived strengths and characteristics of the family.

F2 THE TEN FAMILY COMMANDMENTS

USE

Poorly structured families.

SEQUENCE

Families work out their 'official' and unofficial rules and write them on a piece of paper.

Variation: 'Family Law Book' or 'Family Constitution'.

AIMS

To strengthen the family hierarchy. To make overt unspoken or non-defined rules.

MATERIALS

Paper, pens.

INSTRUCTION

'Each family has its own rules and regulations which are meant to make living together easier. Some of these rules are well known to everyone, even if nobody has ever spoken about them, others have never been mentioned and people are confused. And there is also sometimes a total absence of rules. What rules do you have in your family? Can each family list the rules that do exist or should exist, just a bit like inventing a family constitution or the Ten Family Commandments.'

WORK FOCUS

How are rules made? Who reinforces them? What happens when they are broken? Is there a penal codex? Does the family think of itself as being a monarchy, dictatorship, anarchy, or democracy? How do rules get adapted when children grow older or when family members leave or new ones join?

CRITICAL SITUATIONS

Rigidly structured family with a 'dictator' who silences other members → group discussion about advantages and disadvantages of authoritarian systems.

F3 FAMILY TREES

USE
All families.

SEQUENCE
Each family does their own genogram which should include four generations. Families are encouraged to put at least one adjective to each person, or a whole sentence, relating to personal characteristics, values, myths or problems.

AIMS
To look at family patterns over time. To compare themes and patterns with those emerging in other families.

MATERIALS
Big pieces of paper, colouring pencils.

INSTRUCTION
'We would like each family to draw their own family tree. You can use specific symbols to do that. Write for each person their name, surname, age, job/work, one character trait, as well as problems or illnesses they have had. If there are any very complicated relationships between people, please mark these.'

WORK FOCUS

What do you notice about issues in different generations? How did other people manage a particularly problematic situation? What might grandparents and great-grandparents think about how the family has grown and developed? What, if anything, did each person inherit – and from whom?

CRITICAL SITUATIONS

Family has very limited knowledge of previous generations → speculate about what they might have been like and do a 'virtual' family tree. Ask family to do homework to find out about gaps and missing links.

F4 DREAM HOUSE

USE

All families.

SEQUENCE

Each family does a collage of their dream house and these are compared later.
   Variation: dream family holiday.

AIMS

To think about realistic and unrealistic future scenarios. To consider steps to get there.

MATERIALS

Large paper, magazines (homes, travel), scissors, glue or sellotape.

> **INSTRUCTION**
> 'We would like to invite each family to design their dream house – what does it look like, what sort of rooms and amenities do you need, what furniture and fittings, where should it be located?'

WORK FOCUS

What is important for each family member in terms of privacy, safe spaces, joint rooms, luxury? Can agreements be reached about how to furnish the place? What compromises might need to be made? What do people think about the difference between dreaming your life or living your dream? Which wishes or visions have already been realized, which are never likely to come true?

CRITICAL SITUATIONS

Nightmares instead of dreams are presented → ask for times (in the past) when it was still possible to dream – what did these dreams look like? What is against reviving these again and developing them?

Poverty issues cited for not being able to dream → consider non-material dreams, about hopes and aspirations.

F5 PACKING SUITCASES

USE
Families with migration histories.

SEQUENCE
Each family is told that they suddenly need to leave their home (country) and have to pack one small family suitcase to take a few of the most important things. Families then share their experiences with each other.

AIMS
To highlight processes of intra-familial decision making. To decide what is important for families, across cultures, and what one can leave behind and what not.

MATERIALS
One suitcase for each family (can be painted cardboard boxes). Paper, pens, real or symbolic objects to place in suitcases.

INSTRUCTION
'Imagine that you suddenly need to leave your house and, worse, you need to leave the country on the next plane. You only have one small suitcase for all the important family belongings – perhaps five things for the whole family. Can each family talk about what that might be and write down on a piece of paper what you might wish to take – one piece of paper for each thing you want to take. And place the sheets in the suitcase.'

WORK FOCUS
How were the decisions made? Who has the final say? What can one not put in a suitcase? Can one transport values from one culture to another? What gets lost?

CRITICAL SITUATIONS

Refugee families who have literally lost everything are paralyzed by this task/ game → what would you pack now if you had to leave your life here – what is now important for your future?

F6 MEMORY LANE – OR ANTIQUES ROAD SHOW

USE
All families.

SEQUENCE
Families are asked to look at home for emotionally charged objects and memorabilia and to bring these to the group. They should represent aspects of past family life. Families are then encouraged to talk to other families about the memories which are embodied in these objects.

AIMS
To search for past histories and non-dominant narratives. To address 'unfinished business'.

MATERIALS
Old photos and objects from childhood, such as first shoes, security blanket or transitional objects. Limited number (not more than seven), so as to encourage family to choose and negotiate what to bring.

INSTRUCTION

'The older we get, the more we forget. Often there are memories attached to specific objects, whether it's a dummy, a picture, school reports, presents from grandparents. Next time we would like each family to bring no more than five personal souvenirs or relics, nothing expensive but rather something meaningful, things we value for personal reasons. And then we would like to hear something about the stories which are hidden in these objects.'

Variation: 'Select and bring seven photos which tell a story about you as a family.'

WORK FOCUS

Which memories are evoked? Which good stories come to mind? Is there anything hurtful? How would life be different if one had lost one object? Which objects had you thought of bringing and didn't in the end? What was that about? How did you as a family agree on what to bring and what not?

CRITICAL SITUATIONS

A family has lost everything → they can represent on pieces of paper what they might have wanted to bring.

Extreme emotional reactions → encourage other families to talk about how they managed their particular experiences of loss and how they found hope.

F7 IDENTITY PUZZLES

USE

Disorganized families.

SEQUENCE

One person in each family is 'the puzzle' and the other family members need to 'solve' it. A wooden puzzle game is used as a metaphor to illustrate how one can fit things together.

AIMS

To focus on the specific characteristics of one family member and to co-construct their identity.

MATERIALS

Wooden (hard cardboard) puzzle games (at least ten pieces), sticking paper.

INSTRUCTION

'Sometimes we really have problems knowing who and what other people are really like and also who we are. It can be just like trying to put a puzzle together. There are lots of pieces, but do they fit or not? Here is a puzzle game. Please turn it over so that the pieces are all blank and we can then pretend this is the family member you want to find out about – without asking as she or he will have to be totally silent and just listen. Use the sticking paper to write down something about the person and stick it on the puzzle piece – and keep going until you have covered each piece. Then see how and whether it fits all together and make the puzzle pieces fit. Later we can talk about it with everyone in the room.'

WORK FOCUS

How easy or difficult is it to find descriptors of the person? How can seemingly contradictory parts be fitted in? What does the subject of the puzzle make of it all? How does one work out what people are all about? Who is in a position to do it? How can one fill in blanks or gaps?

CRITICAL SITUATIONS

Negative characteristics prevail and scapegoating takes place → therapist looks for and emphasizes positive characteristics.

F8 MIND SCANNING

USE
All families.

SEQUENCE

Each family member is asked to fill in on the map of a 'brain/mind' (see Figure 4.1) the various holes (and ventricles), speculating about 'what's on the mind' of a family member. Different 'mind scans' of the same person are obtained via the views of different family members.

AIMS

To become curious about the thoughts and feelings of others. To talk about one's ideas of what goes on in other people's minds and to compare this with their own perceptions.

MATERIALS

Paper copies of 'mind/brain' diagram, pens.

INSTRUCTION

'Do you know what this is? It's a kind of brain but it has more holes than we usually have and therefore it's also a mind. You can see that

Figure 4.1 Mind scanning.

some of the holes (doctors call four of them ventricles) are bigger and others are rather small. Imagine that this is your dad's head – put in there what you think his interests are, his likes and dislikes. And I am going to give another brain to your mum – can you, Mrs F, put in there what you think goes on in your husband's head – his interests and his likes and dislikes. You can even put any secrets you think he has in there – maybe in the small holes. And you, Mr F, can you put in this brain diagram here what you think your wife believes goes on in your head. Just scan it. Later we are going to have a look at what goes on in our heads.'

Variation: There are many possible variations. In the above example there are three 'scans' of the same mind/brain. One can be less ambitious and get one person to merely speculate about thoughts and feelings in someone else's head. Specific themes can be given to focus this process down, such as: 'Draw in the fears and hopes. How do you think your son would draw this?'

WORK FOCUS

How well do family members know each other? How might the mind/brain have looked like before the illness/problem? Which holes might one want to shrink? How might one go about it? What did it look like before x happened? How would one want it to look in one year's time?

CRITICAL SITUATIONS

Some group members think too concretely and do not understand the instruction → encourage them to watch members of another family do the exercise and get them to explain the task.

F9 LIFE RIVER

USE

All families.

SEQUENCE

Each family draws their own life river, looking back to the origins and looking into the future where family life flows. Experiences are compared and discussed in the large group. The picture is initially presented by one family member, preferably a child, with the support of the parent. Pinning pictures on the wall helps to have a better overview.

AIM

To review family life from a meta-perspective. To reflect about possible crises and how to navigate these, as well as sharing experiences of how they were navigated in the past.

MATERIALS

Wallpaper roll, colouring pencils, paint.

INSTRUCTION

'It is possible to think about our life as a kind of river, with the springs getting together and forming a little stream which then gets bigger until it is a river. In life, as in rivers, one needs to negotiate new bends, unforeseen obstacles such as rocks and currents. Sometimes the river, our life, flows calmly and then suddenly we are swept along by it. So now imagine that this is your life as a family and you are looking at it from a bird's-eye perspective, or imagine you are sitting on the river bank and see it flowing past you. What do you see? Imagine the river has different parts, beginning from the spring, with the birth of your children – or when you met each other – and ending when it flows into the sea. If new streams flow into the river, like new additions joining the family, then mark these down. And just notice where the river, the family, flows and how it drifts.'

Related techniques: life lines, family chronicles, time lines.

WORK FOCUS

How did the river/life change its course due to external influences? How can one ensure that it remains in its river bed? How does one negotiate dangerous currents and rocks? Which have been mastered and how? What challenges may lie ahead? How can these be dealt with? Was there anything that the other families said that was helpful? What did you perhaps not see in this way?

CRITICAL SITUATIONS

Family focuses only on negative experiences → therapist and other families help to search for positives.

Younger children become restless → each family should not present for more than 15 minutes, or some breaks in between.

F10 GOAL TREES

USE

Particularly useful for poorly structured families.

SEQUENCE

Each family makes a poster with the short- and long-tem goals of each person in the form of a tree. Families then present and compare their trees.

AIMS

To develop future perspectives about life after the problem/illness has gone and to generate hope.

MATERIALS

Large poster paper, colouring pencils or felt pens.

INSTRUCTION

'In this task we would like each family to draw or paint a huge tree – we call this a goal tree. Every person in the family gets a few branches – the big ones are for the important goals both in the near and distant future. The smaller branches are for the smaller goals. Maybe you should also have some big branches – or even the trunk of the tree – for common family goals or goals for the parental couple. Please write your family name at the bottom of the trunk and place a big basket next to the tree.'

Once each family has completed their poster, it is hung on the wall. 'Please take a felt pen and go round and look at these trees and then write one compliment for each family and put it in the basket. We call these baskets "fertilizer buckets" because they are there to strengthen the family to achieve their goals.'

WORK FOCUS

How big, how small and how realistic are these goals? How can they be achieved? What assistance does one need to get there? What are the obstacles to the goals? Which goals have already been achieved? What would be the first small step a person/family could make to get there? Who would need to take which steps?

CRITICAL SITUATIONS

Participants remain stuck in their current problematic situation → therapist does relaxation exercises and takes participants on a fantasy trip to another place and another time.

F11 CONFLICT MAPS

USE

Families with frequent conflicts at home, school or work.

SEQUENCE

Families draw maps of where conflicts occur – maps of their flat/house, maps of their neighbourhood, school, etc. and mark those areas in red where conflicts occur.

AIMS

To discover links between context and problematic behaviours and interactions. To identify conflict patterns and ways of avoiding confrontations in the future.

MATERIALS

Paper, pens, ruler.

INSTRUCTION

'Can each family draw the floor plan of your flat/house. Mark in red where the typical battles/fights/arguments take place. Also do a map of your area, where you are, the neighbours, shops, school, and so on. Also mark where the most problematic behaviours occur.'

WORK FOCUS

How do you explain that your teenage children have most of their arguments outside the bathroom? If you all wanted to reduce these, what would need to happen at home? How come that you and your husband always argue in the bedroom? What would happen if each time you are tempted to have yet another argument, you change the 'scene of the crime' by pausing and moving into another room before continuing to argue? Would a change of 'crime scene' really help? What else could reduce the conflict?

CRITICAL SITUATIONS

Arguments ensue in vivo and escalate → pause and carry out escalation clock exercise (P3).

F12 HYPOTHETICAL SCENARIOS

USE

All families.

SEQUENCE

Therapist and families consider a typical problematic situation. This is enacted, with target family describing scenario and other families experimenting with writing different endings.

AIMS

To rehearse problem situations in imagination, or via role plays, so as to prepare for stressful situations. To experiment with new solutions.

MATERIALS

Props as appropriate to scenarios.

> **INSTRUCTION**
> 'Can you describe a typical situation which usually ends badly. What happens first – and how do things get worse. Now that we all know how it develops, let's stage it. Who would like to play what part? Let's see what one can do differently at what point.'

WORK FOCUS

How did things get stuck? What does one do with an utterly predictable 'script'? How can one write new lines?

CRITICAL SITUATIONS

Target family regards play as unrealistic → invite family to do their own staging or give directions to make it more relevant to target family.

FI3 RESCRIPTING

USE

Multiproblem families, multicultural family groups.

SEQUENCE

Parents with children from another family design two sketches of conflict situations and ensuing arguments, one with a 'typical' outcome and the other with a constructive and surprising ending.

AIMS

To experiment with different outcomes to familiar problem scenarios.

MATERIALS

Props for various scenarios.

WORK FOCUS

How does the problematic situation always end? Who writes this boring script and why do others speak the lines they don't like? Who would need to change for there to be a new script? Which new lines do you suggest?

CRITICAL SITUATIONS

Some group members are hesitant and reluctant to engage in role plays → someone else plays their roles and they may be encouraged to become the 'director' of the sketch.

F14 FAMILY MEAL

USE

Families with eating issues/disorders, chaotic families.

SEQUENCE

Families plan and make a joint meal. This is served and families place themselves round a huge table. Food can be bought together (via supermarket outing) and then be prepared in the work setting, with appropriate childcare arrangements being put in place.

AIMS

To encourage cross-family negotiations and planning. To highlight specific resources and improve group cohesion. To reflect on specific issues around food and mealtimes.

MATERIALS

Food, ingredients, big table.

your children should eat. Make the portions as healthy as you think they should be. We [staff] won't eat with you but we will be around to feed back our observation and any advice, if needed.'

WORK FOCUS

With anorexic teenagers: therapists draw attention to seemingly conflict-avoiding interactions by questioning these: 'Mrs A, do you think that this portion is sufficient for your child to increase her weight? What do other mothers and fathers think? How big should a portion be for a healthy young person? I can see you act as if you think it is okay for your daughter to have only a quarter of the portion you originally agreed on. What do other people here think?'

With 'chaotic' families: 'It has taken you a whole hour and there is still no food on the table for you and the children. They seem very hungry and are very restless – is that okay? If not, what would you need to do to make it happen?'

With multicultural clientele: 'We would like all the families here to think about making a meal together, maybe next week. To make it as rich and diverse as possible, it would be great if each family can bring or make a dish which is typical for the country/culture you come from. You probably need to talk to each other so that you can coordinate a multicultural meal, maybe even make a menu so that everyone knows who does what and how it all fits together.'

And during cooking: 'Some of us still remember what it was like when we spent time with our granny in the kitchen – because grannies and great aunts were often amazing at telling stories over the stove. Who here remembers some of these? Why don't you tell each other stories from where you come from.'

CRITICAL SITUATIONS

Anorexic teenager refuses to eat anything → discussions about the short-term consequences of not eating and then implementing these.

F15 LIFE AFTER A SERIOUS ACCIDENT

USE

Families which had to deal with sudden onset of disorder/problem, or significant losses.

SEQUENCE

Parents and children are separated and the parents are told to imagine that their child has had a serious accident and that from one day to the next the child needs 24-hour care and looking after at home. They are encouraged to devise an emergency plan. The children are asked – in a group taking place in parallel in another room – to imagine that granny broke her hip and that she needs to be looked after at home intensively. Both groups are brought together subsequently and explain their actions and plans. In a subsequent discussion the issue as to whether physical and psychological disorders are similar or different can be tackled.

AIMS

To consider how to activate resources during crisis situations.

MATERIALS

Paper, pens.

INSTRUCTION

'We now want to terrify you a bit by choosing a theme which is particularly scary for parents, but which many families have probably encountered one way or another or have at least contemplated. Imagine your child has had a bad accident and can't move and requires a lot of care and looking after. The hospitals are full and the medical team thinks that you can look after your child at home. The only hope the doctors can give you is that over the next two years your child will make a full recovery, but it's going to take time. Initially you have to work out how to care for your child around the clock. Please work out an emergency plan, maybe in collaboration with one other family, how you are going to manage this situation. Which big and small changes do you need to make – in the family, job, sharing duties and tasks? What help might you access, which personal ambitions do you need to sacrifice?'

Later: 'Can you all now consider how you make emergency and long-term plans with children/adults who have psychological problems/illnesses? How much care does a person need? Who has to make which sacrifices? What changes need to happen? Can friends and others help?'

Later: 'Can each family now, for themselves, make their own specific tailor-made plan as to how to deal with your crisis.'

WORK FOCUS

How did family, friends and the professional network react? Which responses are helpful and which are not?

CRITICAL SITUATIONS

Some parents paralyzed by the very thought of child suffering serious accident → therapist may get them to consider natural catastrophes and their aftermath (floods, earthquakes, fire).

F16 FAMILY PICTURES AND COLLAGES

USE

All families.

SEQUENCE

Each family makes a 'current' family picture together. After presenting this to the other families, they are asked to make a picture of how they would like to be in six months.

AIMS

To provide a snapshot of current family life and a future vision. To see how a family works together, its organization and structure.

MATERIALS

Large pieces of paper, painting utensils, scissors, glue, magazines.

> **INSTRUCTION**
> 'We would like each family to make their own picture of how you see yourselves as a family. Please put such a picture together. You can use colour pens, paint, images from magazines, you can make a collage, whatever you like.'
> *Later:* 'Now make a picture of how you would like to see your family in six months' time.'

WORK FOCUS

What does the picture reveal about how the family works? What are the wishes and hopes? How well did they all work together when making the pictures? Who showed initiative – who didn't? Who has the main 'say'?

CRITICAL SITUATIONS

One person dominates and organizes everyone to adopt his 'vision' → therapist challenges or uses reflecting team.

F17 RELATIONSHIP MAP

USE
All families, during later phases of MFT.

SEQUENCE
Each family or each individual family member constructs their own family relationship map, describing all the relationships between the different members of the family. The maps are then shared in the larger group of families.

AIMS
To highlight hierarchies, boundaries and other family structures.

MATERIALS
Paper, colouring pencils.

INSTRUCTION
'Each family has its own structure and way of managing relationships between its members. We would like each family to map its relationships and structure. Circles and squares can represent female and male family members respectively and their relationships can be drawn with connecting lines. Really strong and close relationships can be drawn with double or treble lines, more distant relationships just with a dotted line. Troubled or adversarial relationships can have some flashes between them, or zigzags. Remember to put in all the people currently living together, or even apart, anyone who is important, including grandparents, uncles and aunts. If you don't know about some of the relationships, speculate about what they might be like. If there are any coalitions between people, invent a symbol to describe this. Maybe also mark the boundaries between different generations and different branches of the family and whether you think these are rigid, flexible or too loose – and don't forget to put yourself in there as well.'

Later: 'If you could only change one of the relationships on this map, which one would you go for first? How could you do that – and if it is changed, which other relationships might change automatically? And in what direction?'

WORK FOCUS
Which relationships are the best, which most painful? What would this map look like if you had drawn it one year ago? What should it look like after therapy? Who is on top of the hierarchy, who at the bottom? Was there a time when this was different? What happened? What are the boundaries like? How

come different members of the same family each draw very different maps – what is this about? What changes would people like to make? If one relationship was less close, what would be different in other relationships?

CRITICAL SITUATIONS

One family member (e.g. father) dominates this exercise → therapist: 'Where would you place your father on this map? Right on top – like a gigantic presence? Is that the way it feels right now? Do you feel okay about that? And what do you imagine the others, on the bottom of the pile, think or feel about this?'

F18 LIFE CIRCLES

USE

Early phase of MFT, particularly with socially isolated families.

SEQUENCE

Each member of each family has three minutes to do their own 'life circle'. These are then presented in a large group or subgroups.

AIMS

To make overt significant people, interests and relationships and to show how these might complement or compete with each other. To think about the implications of change and its effects on relationships of individuals. To draw or construct a schematic diagram of their life – composed of family, friends, interests and passions. It maps, in spatial relationships, people and interests.

MATERIALS

Paper, pens.

INSTRUCTION

'We are interested in each of you, young and old, and how you see your life right now. Let's imagine that this circle stands for your life as it is now (a large circle is drawn to cover most of the paper). We would like you to draw in some smaller circles to represent all the other people important to you – family members, friends, enemies, neighbours, whoever you like. People can be inside or outside this large circle, they can be touching, overlapping or far apart. The circles can be large or small depending on how important people are to you. Anyone you think should be on this piece of paper, alive or not, family or not – just put them in. Do remember to put yourself in as well. Also put in other important areas of your life, such as work, hobbies, your god, or dog, or whatever. Put an initial on each circle so that you can identify it later. And also, and this is important, put the illness – or your symptoms – in the circle – wherever you think they belong. And don't worry how you do it – there are no right or wrong circles, just do it the way you think it is best. Why don't you now take three minutes to do it, just by yourself and we can have a look at it afterwards.'

WORK FOCUS

Would you like to tell me who is who and what is what? How do you like this picture? Are you happy with it? Looking at this picture now, is there anything that strikes you as being surprising? I notice that this circle is very close to that one – can you tell me about that? There seems to be a lot of space between circle A and circle C – is this just a coincidence or would you care to tell me about that? Anything you might want to change – not just in the picture but also perhaps in real life? How would you like it to be different? How could you make that happen? What is that relationship like? What would happen if you got closer to your mother? What if you told your wife that she should talk less to her own mother? How would that change this picture?

CRITICAL SITUATIONS

Family members ask therapists for explanations or interpretations → turn to other families for advice and brainstorming.

F19 STRINGING ALONG

USE

Over-close or distant relationships inside or between families.

SEQUENCE

Ropes are used to connect people and to mark their respective positions and relationships. Families are encouraged to experiment with the ropes.

AIMS

To demonstrate/experiment with distance and closeness between family members.

MATERIALS

Thick string – 10 m; digital camera to take snapshots of the different rope scenarios.

INSTRUCTION

'Here are a few ropes and we want you to use them to show how close and distant you are from each other. It may be the case that you each see this differently and that's why we would like each family member to do their own version. Please hold one end of the rope and give the other end to another family member, maybe the one you think is least close to you. Now place the rest of your family somewhere along the rope – they don't have to be in a straight line. They may not agree – it's just the way you see it. Later everyone can have their turn and we can take a few pictures so that we can remember how people did it and then talk about it.'

WORK FOCUS

How different are the perceptions of relative distances in the same family? What happens if one person pulls? How does that feel? What can one do to change the closeness between two people?

CRITICAL SITUATIONS

Children fight over the ropes and/or behave dangerously → parents are encouraged to exercise their parental responsibilities.

F20 CLAY FAMILY SCULPTURES

USE

All families.

SEQUENCE

All families sit around a huge table and receive instructions on how to make a sculpture of their respective family with the use of self-hardening clay. This can be done separately by each family member, age permitting, or each family can make one joint sculpture. Each person/family subsequently presents their piece to the other families.

AIMS

To represent family relationships and positions as the sculptor sees it at present. To explore possible changes by moving the figures around.

MATERIALS

Self-hardening clay, water, wooden boards to place sculpts on.

INSTRUCTION

'We would like each person/family to use the clay to make a sculpture of your family as you see it now. Make all the members of the family and place them on the wooden board. Make them as big or small as you like, or how important they seem to you. Pay attention to how they are positioned in relation to each other. This can have something to do with their problems or illness, or just how you experience it. And give your sculpture a name or title. You have 30 minutes to complete the task – and afterwards we can pretend that we are in a modern art gallery and each person is presenting their work to the others.'

Each family/person explains their sculpture and its name and reports how and why they made it this way. Other families are invited to comment. It is also possible to turn members of other families into instant art critics: 'We would now like the artists to lean back and listen to the experts on family sculptures. We would like you to pretend that this is your job – an art critic – and that you have to describe and perhaps interpret the sculpture. What are your ideas as to who is in this sculpt and what it all means?'

WORK FOCUS

Which person in this sculpture do you worry about most? If something had to change in this family – where would one start? Where might you place the illness/problem? What would the family look like if the problem/illness was no longer there? Where should something change – who is most and least interested in promoting it? Which of the many relationships might you want to change first? And if you moved that person closer to that one – what would happen to the others?

CRITICAL SITUATIONS

Group members feel incompetent and have difficulties with playing → therapists help actively.

F21 'LIVE' SCULPTING

USE

Unspecific.

SEQUENCE

One family is placed in an inner circle, with all the other group members sitting in an outer circle. The family member with the 'identified' problem/

illness is the sculptor and positions his relatives how he experiences the family now and how he remembers things were in the 'good old days'. The group discusses the differences between the two sculpts and the possibilities for change.

AIMS

To generate new ideas and perspectives about how families have got 'fixed' or may be 'stuck' and to experiment with taking new positions.

MATERIALS

Red and green ropes, each approximately 15 feet long.

INSTRUCTION

Therapist addresses symptomatic/'identified' client: 'Please come with me – you have a unique chance now to sculpt your family – your parents, siblings and other important and relevant persons. You can move them as if they were made out of plasticine or rubber. They will move the way you want them to, but they cannot talk. Find a typical position and posture for each of them. If some of your family members are not here and you think they are important, you can pick persons from other families to stand in. Have a go and I may from time to time ask questions if I am puzzled.'

The therapist surrounds the sculpt area with a red rope which is meant to signify the 'problem area' and explains this: 'Now find a place and posture for yourself in this sculpt. And now I would like all of you to be silent for two minutes and feel the situation. Afterwards I would like you to come out of the sculpt again and someone else from the group here can take your position. So what does it feel like in there – and what does it look like from the outside? Why is this person in that position?'

Later the therapist asks the person to move back into the sculpt and then requests assistance from a member of the observing families: 'Can you help me and interview each person in this sculpt about how they feel and what they think about being in their respective positions? Whether it's painful, whether they feel contorted by having to accommodate to specific requests and so on? If you need help, pick an assistant from the group. If you want to take someone from the family out of the sculpt – do so and replace him or her with someone from the group. Sometimes people find it helpful to look at themselves and their family from the outside.'

Later the therapist will ask the family to leave the sculpt, the red rope remaining in its place. The therapist places a green rope near a window and asks the sculptor: 'Was there a time when you felt good as a family? Maybe during a holiday or when celebrating something or when you played a game or had an outing? Please now sculpt a situation when you and the family all felt well. Place your family here, surrounded by the green rope. Who can look at whom, who can be close to whom? Please all remain in that position for two minutes without saying anything.'

The observing group will be asked to comment and share observations and their own experiences. After this the therapist says: 'Well, that all sounds pretty good, but sadly you as a family are in a different place these days. What would need to change so that you could all move in the direction of the green circle?'

WORK FOCUS

What do you think it is like for each family member to be in these positions? How do others see this family? What would you want them to change – and who would have to change their position first? How is that going to alter the places and roles of other family members? How are roles and positions in your families similar or different?

CRITICAL SITUATIONS

Family member refuses to be sculpted → therapist asks member of another family to 'stand in'.

F22 MOOD BAROMETER

USE

Unspecific.

SEQUENCE

Each family and their individual members describe their mood and overall feelings state. The different family members put in their specific data, with one column for the current state and one for the state they would like to be in. Discussions take place as to how to shift from current to desired future mood, as well as exploring past feeling states and contextual issues.

AIMS

To increase families' awareness of the different feeling states of their members. To discuss what changes need to be made to get to more desirable emotional states.

MATERIALS
Large pieces of paper, colouring pens.

INSTRUCTION
'We have prepared a large sheet of paper for each family, with a vertical and a horizontal line. It's to do with rating your mood and overall feelings right now and in the future. You can see that on the left, the vertical line, there is a scale from −10 to + 10 and in the middle there is the 0 line. This is for each of you to fill in how you feel: −10 means really, really bad – and +10 amazingly well. You will probably put your mood in somewhere in between those two extremes. And then there is the horizontal (0) line – on the left of the vertical line is the past and on the right the future and where the 0 is, that's just now. Can each family member then fill in on how they feel now, with different colours so that you know who is who. And then fill in on the left when you each felt lowest in the past and put a date next to it. And when you have done it, can each of you fill in, on the right of the vertical line, what sort of mood you would like to be in when the work with us is finished or any other date. Once you have all done this, find another family as discussion partner and exchange ideas and experiences. And also think about one point: what would be a small step to lift the mood today – who would need to do what to make it happen?'
Variation: the family has to agree on an overall family feeling state.

WORK FOCUS
Who is/has been aware of whose moods and feelings? Who is oblivious to mood changes? Why might that be? What made it possible to lift the mood in the past? How can one build on past experiences of different feeling states?

CRITICAL SITUATIONS
Unrealistic changes are suggested → group is asked to reflect on appropriateness and the issue of high expectations.

F23 RECONCILIATION

USE
High conflict families.

SEQUENCE
Partners, siblings or parent–child dyads are asked to sit in the middle of a circle made up of other families, opposite each other and touching or holding

each other's hands. A therapist kneels next to each person and each partner is asked to complete somewhat ritualized sentences provided by the therapists. The observing families are asked for their feedback and their own stories of how they manage arguments and subsequent reconciliation.

AIMS

To help families to focus on how to resolve conflicts. To practise forgiveness and reconciliation.

MATERIALS

Two chairs, two therapists.

INSTRUCTION

'Mr and Mrs X, please sit on one chair each and very gently touch each other's hands. I am going to try to support you by placing my own hand underneath yours. I will now say the beginning of a sentence and I would like to ask you, Mr X, to find three possible ways of completing this sentence and to look at your wife whilst you do so. It is important that you use exactly the beginning of the sentence I am providing for you and that you don't change it. Please repeat the following sentence: "What I dislike about you is . . . what I dislike about you is . . . what I dislike about you is . . ." and you, Mrs X, you will just have to listen to it, without responding or commenting. Later we will do the same thing the other way round.'

After both partners have completed this, the focus can shift on to what they like about the other person. Later, both partners are addressed: 'Finally, Mr and Mrs X, can you please each formulate a wish – "I want for us the following . . .".'

WORK FOCUS

How do family members manage very different expectations and wishes? How do they make up? What other ways of making up have people experimented with? Why is forgiveness important?

CRITICAL SITUATIONS

Argument escalates → insist on ritualized course of action.

Partners are silent and cannot think or talk → therapists role play each partner for a few minutes.

Chapter 5

Problem-focused exercises

The exercises in this chapter focus on specific problems and disorders. They can be used particularly with those families where the request for therapeutic help has arisen as the result of concerns over one person – the 'problematic' family member. The exercises also aim to address the effects on the family and larger system in order to encourage families to experiment with viewing their difficulties differently and to develop new strategies.

P1 REMOTE CONTROL

USE
Families with severe control issues.

SEQUENCE
Actual (television or DVD/video) remote controls are distributed to families. They are encouraged to play with these and to steer children and adults.

AIMS
To provide a playful illustration of how people control each other mutually – or not. To consider ways of responding to each other differently.

MATERIALS
Old and redundant remote controls (or symbolic ones made out of cardboard).

INSTRUCTION
'Don't you agree that it is wonderful when we use a remote control and – bang – the TV or DVD works? Just a push of the button and there is a sudden change. If only this was possible in real life, it would simplify many things and then parents could get their children to do exactly as they wanted. And perhaps the children could do the same with their

parents. Or the other way round. Just by pressing a button mum jumps up and does what little darling son wants her to do. Or mum presses a button and the children do exactly as they are told. Well, we have good news for you. We have invented just that type of remote control. Here is one for each family. Try for yourself – point it at me and tell me what you want me to do. [Therapist hands the child a remote control and then does exactly as the child tells him to do.] Who here wants to have a go and see how it works in your family? Who here wants to be remote controlled by their child?'

WORK FOCUS

Who and what could or should one 'programme'? How and when might remote controls be handy? How can one construct invisible remote controls? Do you need a driving licence to be a parent or to remote control children effectively? How is it possible to control others – and when is it desirable? Who should be controlling whom? What is too much and too little control? Does self-control come into this?

CRITICAL SITUATIONS

The person operating the remote control wants to bring the 'controlled' person into difficult, abusive or dangerous situations → group discussion as to whether the remote control licence should be taken away from its operator because of 'dangerous driving'.

P2 DOORMAT

USE

Families with young, 'out of control' children.

SEQUENCE

The parents lie down on the floor and allow the children to walk all over them. The roles are subsequently reversed.

AIMS

To enact how parents feel being used, humiliated and being taken for granted.

MATERIALS

Blankets, cushions, large room.

INSTRUCTION

'Parents often feel like doormats; they feel as though their children literally walk all over them and have no respect. We want to make a game out of this common experience. We suggest that the parents all lie down on the floor and that the children take off their shoes and walk and jump over them. Of course, nobody must get hurt and that's why everyone has to be careful. Dear parents, please remember how you feel when that happens. And you, children, imagine what it's like for your parents.'

Later: 'Now we want to turn the tables. We want the children to lie on the floor and the parents to pretend that they are walking all over their children. And everyone is to remember how that feels!'

WORK FOCUS

What was it like to walk over parents? And what was it like to be trampled on? How did people avoid hurting or getting hurt? What did the children feel when they were in their parents' position?

CRITICAL SITUATIONS

The game becomes increasingly aggressive → therapist 'pauses' the play and gets everyone to reflect on how things got out of hand, possibly by using the escalation clock exercise (see below).

P3 ESCALATION CLOCKS

USE

Family violence, anger issues.

SEQUENCE

Each person is asked to recall one personal experience when things escalated, specifically to do with losing control. A visual representation of an escalation clock is drawn and the process of the escalatory interactions recorded. Each person has to consider how the clock could have been stopped before it was too late.

AIMS

To identify potentially escalatory interactions and to consider techniques to avoid symmetry.

MATERIALS

Paper, colouring pencils.

INSTRUCTION

'From time to time we all get into emotional states when everything seems to spiral out of control and when we feel that we "lose it". At those times we can become more and more angry – and it's the same with the other person(s). It's like a vicious circle, like a roundabout and we just can't jump off. Can you each remember a time when this happened to you in the recent past. In order to work with this we would like each person to draw the face of a big clock, with 1–12 and a line from each figure to the middle so that there are 12 segments. Let us imagine that 12 o'clock stands for it being "too late". This is when you explode or when you all start to fight. Write in that segment what happened – and then wind the clock back, hour by hour, so to speak. Work out what happened just before then (at the imaginary 11 o'clock, but this may have been just seconds before the explosion) and what happened at 10 o'clock – and so on. In this way you can trace back how things escalated – what you did or said and what someone else said and what you said or did before the other person did so – and so on. Write this all in the segments of the clock. Once you have tracked it all back, consider what you might have done differently at each point in the time tracked in order to avoid the escalation. Later you can compare your clocks with those of the other people here in the room.'

WORK FOCUS

What happened? Could you see it coming? How did things escalate? Where were you able to predict what was going to happen? How did she react when you did this? What could you have done differently at, say, 6 o'clock? How often have you felt that you wanted to turn back the clock?

CRITICAL SITUATIONS

Escalation during carrying out this exercise as members of the same family have very different recollections and reconstructions of what appears to be the same event → therapist 'pauses' this escalation and uses the very process that has emerged as an example, encouraging other families to help with drawing the escalation clock together, describing what had just happened.

Family claims that they do not know this situation at all → ask members from other families to join this family as 'consultants'.

P4 SUPERNANNY

USE
Families with young children with behavioural problems.

SEQUENCE
One parent from a family is encouraged to pair up with that of another. Both parents are prepared by the therapist to use an ear-bug/microphone system which allows them to supervise each other when dealing with their respective child(ren). The parents discuss how each of them would want to be supervised by the other, including what can be said and how. The therapist remains with the supervising parent behind the one-way screen, assisting her with considering what input to give to the supervised parent. Such sessions last 10 to 15 minutes and are staged around a typical problem scenario (eating, schoolwork, playing a competitive game). At a later stage the parents swap over and the supervisee becomes supervisor. There is a subsequent reflection session involving both parents and later also their children, as well as the other families.

AIMS
To use clients' resources and competencies to help others. To negotiate how to work in partnership.

MATERIALS
Ear-bug supervisory device, one-way screen or audiovisual link.

INSTRUCTION
'Most of you will probably know the programme *Supernanny* from the television. Well, believe it or not, there are plenty of supernannies here, male and female ones. And we want to give you a chance to show how good you are at helping others with their problematic children. We would like each parent to choose a partner parent – and if you are a two-parent family, choose another two-parent family. Like Supernanny you will be able to watch some problem situation that another family is struggling with and your job is to give advice via an ear-bug to the parent who is struggling with their child. You can work out with each other what sort of input you want to have and one of us will sit with supernanny behind the one-way screen.'

WORK FOCUS
Behind the one-way screen: What do you think the mum in the other room is doing? Why do you imagine she is doing it? What might she be thinking and

feeling now? And what does the child make of how the mum is dealing with him? What might you want to say to help her? What sort of responses do you expect?

After the session: How useful did you find the input? What did you learn? What was not helpful?

To children: Did you notice anything different that your mum/dad did? How do you explain this? Was it better or worse?

CRITICAL SITUATIONS

Parent behind the one-way screen seizes up → therapist asks parent what he or she would do, or provides alternatives of what other 'supernannies' might have considered, inviting the parent to think which of these might be useful.

P5 HIT OR SMACK?

USE
Family violence.

SEQUENCE
A doll is used for parents and children to demonstrate what is 'smacking' and what is 'hitting' and to speculate about the effects of physical chastisement.

AIMS
To demonstrate and reflect on the impact of physical force and search for alternatives.

MATERIALS
Big doll (size of baby).

INSTRUCTION
'Many parents believe that there is nothing wrong with smacking their child occasionally if the child misbehaves. Sometimes parents are hit or kicked by their children. Often there are discussions about whether any form of physical chastisement is allowed or not. At other times people argue about the difference of a smack and a hit and whether it needs to hurt a bit or not for the child to get the message. Here is a big doll which of course can't feel any pain. We would like each of you to show how you might smack the doll if she were naughty – and also to show the difference between a smack and a hit.'

WORK FOCUS

What is 'too much' and what is 'too little' chastisement? What do children learn from the parents via physical punishments? What memories, good and bad, do the parents have from their own childhood with respect to receiving physical punishments? How might children's minds be affected by hitting or smacking? What might be the advantages and disadvantages of alternative disciplinary measures?

CRITICAL SITUATIONS

Minimization → therapist asks other families about examples of negative experiences of being hit or smacked.

Parent feels bad and guilty → discussion as to how he or she can feel better: 'What might you avoid in the future? Who could help you so that you don't lose you cool in the future?'

P6 JOB HUNT

USE

Any families where there is a perceived or real disability or disorder.

SEQUENCE

Each person writes a reference for one of its family members, emphasizing positives. They can then match this 'job description' (and/or person specification).

AIMS

To look for positives in each other. To match individual characteristics with desired qualities.

MATERIALS

Paper, pens.

INSTRUCTION

'Can everyone think of one person in your family and imagine they want to apply for a job. What sort of a reference might you want to write to support the job application? Write what's positive but also what's true – otherwise they won't get the job. You can ask other people in the group to point out some of the positives if you find it difficult to think about these yourself.'

WORK FOCUS

How difficult was it to find positives? How did you account for people's difficulties or problems? How do you manage praise and criticism in your family? When is praise important? Should you mention negative aspects of a person or family? What are the advantages and disadvantages of criticism?

CRITICAL SITUATIONS

Illiterate parents → therapist/other adult becomes scribe.

P7 FOOD COLLAGES

USE

Anorexia nervosa, multiproblem families.

SEQUENCE

Each member of each family is asked to compose a symbolic meal, made up of cut-outs from food journals. These are placed on plates and later presented. Explanations are given about each plate and how decisions were reached.

AIMS

To reflect on eating/food and typically arising conflicts, anxieties and fantasies. To experiment with playful interactions around eating.

MATERIALS

Plates, food magazines, scissors, sellotape, glasses, bowls.

INSTRUCTION

Variation 1 (one plate for parents, one for young person): 'Dear parents, please make the Sunday lunch for your child. We have plates and food magazines and you can cut out the food that you think your daughter and the family should eat. Cut out all the ingredients of the food, in real size portions and stick these on the plate. And you, young people, to make your own meal, what you would like to eat next Sunday for lunch?'

Variation 2 (one plate for each family member): 'Mr J, please put on this plate the Sunday lunch which you think your wife would like to prepare for your daughter. And you, Mrs J, can you put on your plate the meal that you think your husband would like to prepare for your daughter. And you, Jane, can you put on your plate the meal that you think your mother would like to serve you. Next you, Mrs S. Can

> you put on your plate the meal that you think your daughter would like you to make for her. And you, Mr S, could you put on your plate the meal that you think your daughter believes you would want your wife to make for her.'

WORK FOCUS

What do you make of all these different Sunday lunches – which fits 'best'? With this plate, will there be plenty of arguments? Who will give in first? How much would she need to eat for you to feel that she is putting on weight rather than losing more? If she doesn't eat her lunch on Sunday, what is going to happen? Do you think your parents are over the top to expect you to eat all this? How do you explain that they think that this is what you should eat? Who is right and who is wrong?

CRITICAL SITUATIONS

Young person does not want to do task → therapist: 'Is this your daughter talking now, or is it anorexia making yet another speech. If you give in, which part of your daughter might you be supporting, the healthy or unhealthy part?'

P8 ADOPTIVE MEAL

USE
Anorexia families, multiproblem families.

SEQUENCE
Parents and children are swapped over during a lunchtime meal.

AIMS
To help parents to gain the experience of being more successful with getting the child of another family to eat. To discover resources they have not used when dealing with their own child. To let 'adopted' children experience different forms of being parented.

MATERIALS
Food and eating utensils.

> ### INSTRUCTION
> 'Today we want each set of parents to "adopt" another child to see how lunch works out. Afterwards the children will be returned to their real

parents. Please pick another child from the group. You are responsible for this child now for the next hour or so, but if you are a bit uncertain you may ask the real parent for some advice or tips. Just ensure that the child does not sit next to their natural parent, so that all the members of the new family can get into conversation.'

WORK FOCUS

What worked with the other child and what didn't work? What did you notice about your own child and his 'adoptive' parents – how did they do? How do you explain the differences? How was lunch with the other family for you?

CRITICAL SITUATIONS

Child/teenager refuses to eat and 'adoptive' parents are helpless → get advice from children of other families.

P9 ANONYMOUS LETTERS

USE

Unspecific, but only once there is good group cohesion.

SEQUENCE

Group members put beside the name of each person one or more characteristics, in the form of praise or constructive criticism. The handwriting is changed so as to anonymize the author. The anonymous letters are then all collected by the therapist and redistributed and read out aloud. If the reader receives his or her own letter, they pass it on to someone else without drawing attention to themselves.

Variation: the therapists are also listed as group members on the piece of paper and participate.

AIMS

To explore covert thoughts and feelings about others. To discuss the pros and cons of openness and transparency.

MATERIALS

Paper (containing all the names of group members in vertical order), pen.

INSTRUCTION

'You have known each other for a few weeks now. Here is a piece of paper which contains all the names of the group members. We would like you to write beside each name, including your own name, one observation. This could be praise, constructive criticism or some form of encouragement. It has to be something personal that you want to give him or her. Please change your handwriting so that nobody can recognize who the author of the anonymous letter is. Later we will read these anonymous letters out aloud.'

WORK FOCUS

What is new, what is surprising information? What can one say openly, what can one only say anonymously? Why is this the case? What would need to be different for people to say openly what they think and feel about another person?

CRITICAL SITUATIONS

Too much focus on negatives → therapist uses 'magnifying glass' to look for strengths.

Participants are unable to write → members of other families are asked to be the 'scribe' and 'reader'.

P10 MASKS

USE

Adolescents and their families with sense of hopelessness about the future.

SEQUENCE

Adolescents choose paper masks and are asked to play themselves, meeting up in 60 years' time and exchanging their lifetime experiences. The therapist, without a mask, initially interviews each adolescent until a spontaneous conversation emerges. The parents listen to this in an outer circle and are asked subsequently to become a reflecting team via a 'goldfish bowl' activity.

AIMS

To develop future vision and think about hypothetical futures from which they construct their lives retrospectively.

MATERIALS

Table, tea and cakes, masks.

INSTRUCTION

The therapist starts the role play by letting each young person take a mask and sit down around a table for an improvised tea party. As the party starts, the parents are invited into the room and they are asked, without explanation, to place themselves silently in an outside circle, as mere observers. The therapist greets all the 'old' ladies and gentlemen: 'I am ever so pleased that after 60 years you have all come back here. We last saw each other here in 2010 – I have literally forgotten your names – what are your full names now? I think I remember meeting your first husband at some stage. How many children and grandchildren do you have now? And in your case, how many marriages and divorces have you had? Do you still suffer from an eating disorder (ADHD, depression)? Did you ever go to university or did you end up in Hollywood right away?'

With such invitations the adolescents usually invent all sorts of dramatic stories and prospective 'CVs' and the therapist encourages interactions between the teenagers. At a later stage the therapist can ask further questions: 'Do any of you still live in England? Are your parents still alive? What is (has been) your relationship like? If you think back, what or who helped you most in the days after you came here, all these years ago?'

Later: 'Let us imagine that we are now in the year 2040 – you are all middle-aged – see whether you might have a similar conversation. And now we want you to be in the year 2020.'

WORK FOCUS

When you look back on your life, what were the turning points? Which of the stories might come true? What might you need to do to get there? What do you, parents, make of what you have heard? What do you, young people, think about what the parents have said about your role play?

CRITICAL SITUATIONS

Teenagers find it difficult to get into role → therapist becomes very active and set the scene and persists in addressing each person in role.

P 11 LETTER TO PROBLEM/ILLNESS

USE

Diagnosed disorders, such as anorexia nervosa, Asperger syndrome, ADHD and others.

SEQUENCE

All group members write one positive and one negative letter to 'the problem' (illness, disorder). The letters all get put together and are then distributed in such a way that each group member receives a positive and negative letter (not their own). These are then read, one by one, starting with the negative ones first.

AIMS
To examine positive and negative feelings and thoughts the problem has evoked.

MATERIALS
Pencils, paper.

INSTRUCTION
'We would like to ask each of you to write two letters. The first one should start like this: "Anorexia (ADHD), I hate you because ..." List about ten points why you hate this illness/problem. Parents write this from your point of view and the young people can write separately about the negative aspects. The second letter should start: "Anorexia, I am grateful to you because ..." This letter must not be sarcastic, but also contain ten points outlining the positive changes in your life which the illness has brought you.'

Later: 'Now that we have mixed up all the letters, we will distribute them and they can be read out loud. Let's start with the negative ones.'

WORK FOCUS
What are the concerns and pressures that the problem produces? Which positive changes has the problem inadvertently created?

CRITICAL SITUATIONS
Symptom bearers glorify their own problems, or get stuck in negative experiences → therapists challenge negative frames by encouraging other families to challenge these.

P12 TRICKS AND KNACKS

USE
Specific disorders, specifically addictions.

SEQUENCE
Exchange of information about the 'shadow' sides of a specific disorder and the tricks the disorder plays.

AIMS

To make transparent and look at the problem as being separate from the person (*'Anorexia does this, not my daughter'*) and not as an attack on relatives. To reduce the helplessness of relatives by looking at the illness in its own right and its effects on the person (*'Is this the illness or is it our son speaking?'*).

MATERIALS

Personal experiences of all group members.

INSTRUCTION

'Over the next hour we want to examine the "nasty" aspects of your son's disorder by exchanging ideas and information you have all collected over the years. In order to fight the problem, you need to understand it. So let's start by collecting ideas about what you have noticed and how that might be related to the illness. You can all write a scientific paper or make a documentary movie about the illness and how it affects the sufferer – including all the tricks it plays!'

WORK FOCUS

One may consider working initially in two parallel groups – adolescents and parents.

Substance misuse: which specific tricks does the addiction employ at home – how to get money (stealing money, valuables, borrowing money from siblings, plundering savings), hiding substances or alcohol, denial of being intoxicated?

Anorexia nervosa: which tricks does anorexia play – manipulation, deception, including weighing strategies (wet hair, drinking water before), hyperactivity (sport, cold showers), vomiting, diets, hiding food?

Variation: a film can be scripted and shot made by all group members, illustrating visually 'the tricks anorexia plays'.

CRITICAL SITUATIONS

Over-reaction by anxious parents (*'You give them the wrong ideas'*) → ask these parents to prepare a 'secret dossier' on the illness or disorder and then share this with other parents, before considering discussing its content with adolescents.

P13 BODY IMAGE POSTERS

USE

Adolescent anorexia nervosa, bulimia nervosa, obesity.

SEQUENCE

Subjective and objective pictures of body image are made (about 30 minutes) and subsequently compared.

AIMS

To demonstrate, above all to parents and other relatives, the body image distortion of anorexia nervosa sufferers. To help parents gain an understanding that their daughter's body image distortion has the quality of a delusion which cannot be challenged rationally. To help parents to consider what responsibility they themselves need to take in the face of this illness-related delusion.

MATERIALS

Paper rolls (wallpaper), felt pens, bluetack, measuring tape.

INSTRUCTION

Parents and children of the same sex (e.g. mothers and daughters, fathers and sons) work together. There are two body image drawings for each anorexia sufferer. To get the first poster, the therapist says, after marking on the paper roll the real length of the young person's body: 'Please draw your own body on this roll, just as you perceive it and feel it. It should represent how you think you look, without any clothing.' For the second poster, the anorexia sufferer is asked to strip down to their underwear and to lie on the paper roll. The instruction for the parent is: 'Please draw the outline of your daughter, very tight along the contours of her body, and do hold the pen absolutely vertical and straight.'

WORK FOCUS

Which are the 'problem zones' of the body which the teenager can accept? Which are difficult to cope with? When using a measuring tape, what are the differences between the subjective and objective body image? Who can you trust to do that? Who should nominate the person, the teenager or parent? How does body image distortion become a driving force? Can the anorexia sufferer 'correct' their distorted view of themselves and what might be the consequences of this 'delusion' for the teenager's ability to eat normally? What about personal freedom and the right to die?

CRITICAL SITUATIONS

Anorexia sufferer minimizes differences → therapist turns to girl's own parents and to other parents, asking them whether they agree.

P14 PRESS CONFERENCE/TALK SHOW

USE
Specific problems or disorders in children and teenagers.

SEQUENCE
Children and parents are separated into two groups, with the children preparing for the role as 'world experts' on a specific disorder/illness. Meanwhile the parents formulate specific questions. This is followed by a staged television interview/talk show with parents interviewing children.

AIMS
To place children in an expert role, talking about the illness/disorder. To allow parents and children to gain some distance from their own personal situations and to meta-communicate about the general issues raised by illness.

MATERIALS
Desk, chairs and props such as mock-microphone, bottle of water and glass for speaker, white coat.

INSTRUCTION
'Can we make two groups, one for children and one for the parents, with the children coming to this room please and the parents staying here.'

To children: 'We want to ask you to help us to direct a television programme called "Help, My Child Has . . ." (ADHD, anorexia, Asperger syndrome, etc.). You are the experts on this problem, maybe a famous doctor and a scientist or researcher, and you should talk expertly about this topic, maybe quoting from your latest books and research studies. You will each have a name displayed in front of you, such as Prof Dr Dr Clever. Please answer the questions which are put to you as constructively as you can, and if you cannot answer a question pass it on to another member of the panel.'

To parents: 'You are the audience for a television programme called "Help, My Child Has . . ." and I am directing the show. Over there, at the long table, are all the experts. You, as the audience, have the unique opportunity to ask these highly competent experts all the questions which have been preoccupying you all these years. Here, Mrs A, is the microphone, please do ask the first question.'

WORK FOCUS
What is known about a specific illness? What do experts know – and what don't they know? Does one need experts? What for? How did the

parents experience their own children? What can one do to find answers to questions?

CRITICAL SITUATIONS

Child cannot let go of patient role → ask other panel member to comment on the child as a typical example of displaying the illness or disorder and interview child in the role of 'expert by experience'.

P15 THIRD BREAKFAST

USE

Anorexia nervosa, other families with eating or feeding issues.

SEQUENCE

Role reversal between parents and children. The adolescent (in the role of a parent) feeds the 'third breakfast' (at about 11.00, assuming there has already been a very early breakfast and a snack at about 10.30) to a reluctant parent (in the role of a child). If the adolescent does not succeed in this task, she has to eat the breakfast.

AIMS

To thematize feeding and eating issues in a playful manner. To highlight and address conflicts arising around food and eating.

MATERIALS

Sandwich, drink, napkins.

INSTRUCTION

Three families are being placed in observer positions. 'Please observe carefully what happens next and note down the best arguments of the Brown family. You, Emily, should play your mother and you, Mrs Brown, you need to play your daughter.'

Variation 1 (anorexia nervosa) – to mother (in role of daughter): 'You are Emily and 16 years old [followed by brief description of person]. You have been ill for years and you are at present in outpatient treatment and find a third breakfast totally unacceptable. As an experienced eating disordered teenager you must do anything and everything to prove to your mother that you are not going to eat this third breakfast. Do anything you can to convince your mother, once and for all, that she would never again want to serve you a third breakfast.'

To daughter (in role of mother): 'You are Mrs Brown, 39 years old, and your daughter has worried you for years because of her eating disorder. You have come to the clinic and observed all sorts of things, but on this occasion the therapists have thought about a little exam for you. Your task is to convince your "daughter" Emily, to eat the third breakfast. Use all your maternal abilities and tricks to make this happen. You can use the most unorthodox and surprising methods. In the event that you do not manage to get her to eat the third breakfast, you have to eat it yourself!'

Variation 2 (multiproblem families) – *to one parent:* 'Imagine you are a nine-year-old boy. You don't want to sit at the table when eating, you play with your food, you make the most awful noises and do everything to shock your parents. Any moment now your dad is going to blow a fuse and explode.'

To child: 'You are Alex's dad. He is eating and does everything to annoy you. Your job is to get him to eat the food, with the right manners, without screaming or hitting him. What you should aim for is to have a peaceful meal together.'

WORK FOCUS

What does it feel like to be in role? What new perspectives might have been gained? What was comfortable about being in different role – and what was not?

CRITICAL SITUATIONS

Parents 'ham up' their role as ill child, children become very aggressive in the role as their parent → therapist pauses action and asks other families to comment.

P16 POSTERS AND FILMS

USE

Teenagers with specific presentations.

SEQUENCE

Young persons, in groups of two or three, devise a poster/short film to illustrate a particular theme – 'What Is Normal and Where Does Madness Start?'; 'ADHD or Just Bad Behaviour?'; 'What Makes Us Happy and What Makes Us Sad'; 'What Makes Us Feel Good and What Doesn't?' The finished product is later presented to the group of parents and discussed.

AIMS

To help young persons to have the opportunity to represent their views, issues, feelings.

MATERIALS

Large pieces of paper, pens, video camera, disorder-specific props.

> **INSTRUCTION**
>
> 'Over the next hour please make a poster/film about the following theme. Remember that your parents do not know your innermost feelings and thoughts. If you are able to find creative ways to represent the problem and related themes, then maybe your parents will be better able to understand you and they won't always put their foot in it.'

WORK FOCUS

How is it possible to communicate about specific problems? How does one make one's thoughts and feelings intelligible to others? Can parents respect the young person's preoccupations?

CRITICAL SITUATIONS

Young person feels stuck or paralyzed → make poster about this state of mind.

P17 PSYCHO-SELF-EDUCATION

USE

Any diagnosed disorder, illness or disturbance (e.g. schizophrenia, anorexia nervosa, ADHD, Asperger syndrome, diabetes, alcohol and other forms of substance misuse etc.).

SEQUENCE

Families and their individual members are encouraged to pool their knowledge about a specific topic and then provide their expert account.

AIMS

To empower families to become responsible for understanding their difficulties rather than having these explained by experts.

MATERIALS

White coat, access to information, including internet, books.

INSTRUCTION

'Dear families, all of you here in this room have very similar disorders/ illnesses. If one does have such illnesses one needs to know the facts; for example, the symptoms, the reason for treatments, the medication and its side effects, how the body responds, not to mention what those near and dear can do to help, or signs that a relapse might be eminent, etc. Since these are illnesses, some of you may well think that only doctors know about it – but that isn't true in our experience. We have found that if you families all put your heads together and pool your knowledge, then your expertise can help us to understand what it is like to live with the illness. Who here knows something about anorexia nervosa? What do you know about its causes and treatment? Just say or shout out aloud what you know and I will write this up on the flipchart.'

Later: 'Well there are plenty of ideas here. Which of you would like to give a formal lecture on this subject? Here is a white coat – we need a professor [encourage children/teenagers] to sum it all up – so much easier to do so in the white coat of the expert.'

Later: 'Which of your questions have still not been answered? Who might have the relevant information? How could you get it? Here is a laptop and the internet, just in case you might want to use it.'

WORK FOCUS

Who here knows anything else about this issue/matter? How can you find out about this disorder/illness? Who can talk to whom about this?

CRITICAL SITUATIONS

Families construct wrong information regarding medical facts → therapists bring their own knowledge.

Generating new exercises

There is a seemingly infinite number of exercises and many readers will have their own stock of activities and related practices, many of which no doubt can be adapted to multi-family work. Others will want to follow these exercises religiously when starting MFT. We recommend that this is not done in too rigid a way, as the very point of these exercises is to encourage experimentation and playfulness, not only for families but also for professionals.

How can one invent new exercises? We suggest that you think of a 'prop', such as a wig, bottle opener, rope, thermometer – or whatever. Agree with your team which props to use and experiment, first yourselves, in mini role plays with colleagues and friends. Form a number of small 'buzz groups' (two or three persons) which can each be given the task of inventing a multi-family activity around this prop. 'Wild' ideas must be encouraged! Each group should develop their own ideas during a period of no more than ten minutes – the time pressure generally has the effect of focusing the minds of all concerned. Maybe people need to think of ideas which initially only address intra-family issues.

Once each buzz group has shared their ideas with the rest, a relevant multi-family exercise or game can be constructed by the team, pooling ideas and resources. It is also possible to think of a particular activity or game and to translate this to an MFT context. For example, consider doing an exercise entitled 'family vehicle'. This involves drawing a large (public transport) vehicle – boat, bus, aeroplane, train – on which the family embarks to travel together through life. Who sits where? Who is in the driving seat, who sits at the back, and so on? Turn this into a full-blown exercise, with aims, sequence, work focus, etc. Or get each family to design a family board game, with dice and figures and cards with instructions if the figure arrives at a specific field. Suggest a positive theme for the game (e.g. trust, respect, love, 'king or queen for the day') and consider a 'prize' for the loser, such as having to do an unpleasant household chore – this keeps people motivated to wanting to win. Let each family play their game and later swap them over. Think of what to do next.

Chapter 6

Working with multiproblem families

This chapter introduces a number of different projects that have been developed by our respective teams in England and Germany. It addresses problems and difficulties commonly encountered in the work with multiproblem families.

Calling a family a 'multiproblem family' is, of course, not a clinical diagnosis or category, but a convenient label to describe multiply disadvantaged and marginalized families that present with severe relationship problems. Poverty, unemployment, social isolation, educational failure, alcohol and substance misuse and intra-family violence, including child abuse and neglect, as well as severe psychiatric or behavioural disorders, are often all present at the same time. These families have a particular susceptibility to psychological, physical and psychosomatic symptoms and illnesses that is significantly higher than in the normal population. It is often their children who come to the notice of social services, the education authorities, and child and adolescent mental health services. Multiproblem families are frequently also 'multi-agency families', as they have a tendency to attract multiple helpers who provide different and at times contradictory inputs, causing problems in their own right. There is a distinct pattern, in that the family's seeming helplessness paralyzes the professional network, with chronically entrenched relationships developing. With a large number of helpers present, there is usually also a large number of opinions and inputs, which may further contribute to the seeming helplessness and confusion that the families and their individual members experience. They can feel inhibited by the helpers' continued availability and this can create problems in their own right. Increased dependence on expert advice can lead to further helplessness.

In the 1970s, Alan Cooklin and his team at the Marlborough Family Service in London (Asen *et al.* 1982; Cooklin *et al.* 1983) started experimenting with using MFT in their work with multiproblem families. It had been the rather poor results obtained with seemingly 'chaotic' and 'treatment-resistant' families that called for a new approach. This consisted of putting six to eight seemingly 'impossible' families together under one roof, on a daily basis and for months, in a kind of therapeutic community of dysfunctional families. All those years ago it felt rather risky to put such deeply dysfunctional families all 'in the same boat' together. The idea then was that, by undertaking much of the work themselves, the families would become more self-responsible and the clinicians and other helpers would be less central. A highly structured daily programme with deliberately built-in controlled crisis situations, similar to those they might encounter in their everyday lives in their homes, forced these families to address daily living issues in a therapeutic context. The aim was to enable them to identify new forms of self-help and crisis management which no longer required the involvement of an ever-increasing number of professionals. The Marlborough Family Day Unit (FDU), an 'institution for change' (Cooklin et al. 1983), was founded more than 30 years ago and several thousand children and their families have been treated there since.

At the outset, the work of the FDU was very intensive and long: families attended eight hours per day, five days per week, often over a period of many months if not a whole year. However, over the years the approach has undergone many changes and transitions, with therapeutic work now lasting on average 12 weeks and providing a balance between clinic-based and home-based work. Families attend initially for three or four days one week, for six hours, and subsequently less frequently, with home-based work to facilitate the transfer of experiences made in the clinic context to the home environment. This is followed by another intensive three or four whole days within the space of one week (Asen et al. 2001). The FDU acts as a kind of 'pressure cooker', providing intensive whole-day experiences, with much exposure to other families.

The team also discovered that this kind of family work required a new type of therapist, namely professionals who were not there primarily to 'treat' families but to assist them to make use of their own and other families' resources. Furthermore, the therapists had to be 'mobile', having the ability to work in close physical proximity (Stevens et al. 1983) as well as the capacity to distance themselves. They have to be 'on the move', joining with families and activating and then disengaging at the first possible moment. This proved to be quite difficult for therapists who had received traditional trainings. When faced with families who had acquired a 'consumer' position over the years, sitting back and letting therapy and other interventions happen, therapists often struggled not to do more of the same and not to be 'too helpful'. Learning this has not been an easy lesson and it may well have accounted for the initially long spells that families spent in the FDU, reminiscent of a prolonged stay in a sanatorium rather than being placed in a pressure cooker.

Intensive MFT in day settings is a challenge not only for the families but also for the staff. It is highly structured (Asen et al. 1982), with precise timetables and frequent transitions from one activity to the next, from one working context to another. This requires not only family members but also staff to change their roles and tasks within a very short timespan, resulting in each person having to continuously change perspectives and assume new positions. When families arrive in the FDU each morning, they first have some (unstructured) time for themselves. The parents are told that they are entirely responsible for their own children – and that it is not the staff's job to ensure their safety. In fact, a formal ritual in the beginning and at the end of each day can dramatize this, particularly if foster carers or social workers are legally responsible for the children. In such cases the children live away from their parents and they are brought to the FDU in the morning and collected from there in the afternoon. This can lead at times to rather emotional encounters between parents and foster carers. It allows observation of parents' abilities to prioritize their children's needs above their own and whether they can protect their children from their own emotional highs and lows. A planning meeting at the beginning of each day serves for each family to discuss and plan how they are going to use the day in order to address the issues that they want to work on – or that the referring person has identified. As many families portray themselves as victims of social workers and similar authorities, initially they often lay all the blame at social services' door. The question 'What can you do to get rid of your social workers?' can in these circumstances help to focus on concrete goals. If stuck, other families can make helpful suggestions, such as 'You could try and play with your child all day and not be so negative all the time' or 'Show that you are a good parent and make sure that your child always knows where you are' or 'Try and stop your child today from whining and being so attention seeking.' During their attendance, families have a structured timetable (Table 6.1) which requires them to make frequent transitions and changes throughout the day. There are formal groups, involving at various times all attending families together and at other times parents and children separately. There is a mixture of action-oriented and reflective work. A major principle of this work is openness and transparency, not only between the families but also between staff and families. The Family Day Unit is well equipped with cameras, and this allows for family interactions to be recorded and be replayed during video (or DVD) feedback sessions when families view themselves and reflect on their inter-actions. Families can also take small DVD cameras home and make a 'home

Table 6.1 Family day unit (FDU) timetable for Tuesday

9.00 Families arrive
9.30 Planning meeting
10.00 Single family activity
11.00 Reflective round
11.15 MFT activity
12.00 Preparation of lunch, eating and clearing up
13.30 MFT activity
14.45 Reflective round
15.30 Finish

movie' about their life or specific issues. These may then be shown to the whole group of families who can often be more expert at analysing and commenting than extensively (and expensively) trained professionals. In this way families and their individual members become 'consultants' to other families. They support each other, but they also comment on unhelpful patterns they see in each other. Families and their individual members form friendships and create a network of support for isolated families outside of the programme. Experienced 'graduate' families may make themselves available to engage new and sceptical families, offering advice and hope.

After the planning meeting, each family gets involved in an activity, but only with its own members. This can consist of playing a game (Monopoly, Snakes and Ladders), reading a book or carrying out homework set by the school, making a family picture or collage about a holiday they would like to embark on. All these activities require the family members to work together, for someone to lead the play and ensure that there is enough taking of turns. During this time the therapists observe from the 'eagle position' and may approach a family briefly to share an observation or make a suggestion, only to withdraw again and leave the family to itself. In a subsequent reflective round families tell each other what they have done and also what they may have observed, not only about their own interactions but also those in other families. Often a theme emerges which can then be explored in a subsequent multi-family activity. Typical themes are: 'being excluded', 'dominating everything', 'nobody is in charge', 'nobody ever listens', 'good to be together'. Exercises, as described in the preceding three chapters, will be suggested by staff to work and explore the theme.

Around midday each family prepares its own lunch. Families bring their own food and there is a possibility to store supplies for a whole week or longer in lockers and a large fridge. The preparation of food and the actual process of cooking food whilst having to supervise small children can also be stressful and replicate typically difficult domestic situations. The same can be said about washing up and clearing up afterwards. There are often complex interactions between families concerning sharing kitchen utensils or discussing who made a specific 'mess' and who should be responsible for clearing it up. Going on a shopping trip together is a good opportunity to observe how parents manage their at times very challenging children in public, be that on public transport, in shopping centres or supermarkets. Not infrequently, problematic family scenarios are spontaneously enacted and this is an excellent chance for families to share their observations, to suggest different solutions and to help each other out. The outings can be filmed, preferably by one or two of the clients, since they often have quite a different focus. Specific interactions can be viewed and reflected upon in a video feedback session later that day. During the afternoon there is the opportunity for other activities, usually involving all families together, such as games and exercises. At the end of each day there is a brief reflective round, when experiences and observations are shared and goals for the next few days set, including how to transfer the 'lessons' learnt in the FDU to each family's own home.

Once every two weeks there is a more structured reflective round, lasting for most of the afternoon. This 'reflections meeting' (see Table 6.2) is inspired by 'reflecting team' practices (Andersen 1987). It starts with the team of family day unit workers, at present four staff, who convene a clinical meeting which is videotaped. In this clinical meeting the family workers exchange information and views about each family's dynamics, summarizing strengths and weaknesses observed during the previous weeks. This meeting lasts about 30 minutes and the videotape recording is given to another member of the Marlborough team who has not been part of the clinical meeting. This sys-temically oriented clinician meets with all the parents (usually 10 to 12) to watch the videotape of the clinical meeting and to take note of the staff's views, opinions and reflections. The remote control for the video-recorder is given to one of the parents or other adults, a message that it is up to them to let the specific tape segment run for its entirety or to pause, so that specific points can be taken up. Most parents opt for stopping and restarting the tape, as pausing the tape allows family members to respond immediately to the staff's views and reflect on these. It is the systemic clinician's task to get families to become curious about each other and to encourage them to pro-vide advice, criticism and support for one another. During the 'reflections meeting' the family day unit workers are not present in the room, but watch the meeting through a one-way screen. This has the effect of staff being placed in a 'pure' observing position, having to listen to the 'reflections' that families make about their own 'reflections'. In this way staff become temporarily unavailable for being drawn into prolonged discussions with families, such as justifying their views. Instead they listen to the families' reflections without being able to immediately 'put the record straight'. The parents in turn are encouraged by the systemic clinician working with them to speculate on how staff might digest their reflections. The 'reflections meeting' is a popular event, at times more so with families than with staff. Families like the idea

Table 6.2 Reflections meeting

Stage 1 Staff clinical discussion (30 minutes)
Stage 2 Parents' review and reflections (2 hours)

- initial speculations
- first video segment shown
- parents pause and reflect
- inter-family discussion
- next segment, and so on.

Stage 3 Staff reflect on families' reflections (1 hour)
Stage 4 Families reflect on staff's reflections (1 hour)
Stage 5 Staff reflect on families' reflections on staff's reflections (ongoing).

that not only they themselves but also staff can be observed at work. This adds considerably to the ethos of openness and transparency prevailing in the family day unit. A subsequent 'post-reflections meeting', involving the systemic consultant and staff only, creates yet another layer of context: staff reflect on the families' reflections of the staff's reflections. And, to continue with the circular model, staff will let the families know about these reflections, prompting the families to reflect on them – and so on.

Over the past 30 years the Marlborough Family Day Unit in London has pioneered the establishment of the first permanent multiple family day setting, specifically designed for and solely dedicated to the work with seemingly 'hopeless' families. It has resulted in a significantly improved engagement with seemingly impossible families and helped to neutralize poor 'chronic' relationships with professionals. Whilst the main emphasis is on multiple family work, other therapeutic interventions are also used if and when required, such as single family work and individual interventions, including psychodynamic work. 'Supernanny' is a specific technique designed to help parents discover and develop their own resources and to assist each other in managing to 'tame their toddler' or older 'monster' child. This involves the use of a one-way mirror, earpieces and microphone, not unlike the set-up in the well-known television series. However, there is no expert professional supernanny. Instead, parents take it in turns to play that role. Families choose a partner family and the parents discuss among themselves the specific behaviours of their child which they want to address. Staff will assist and help parents to choose appropriate partners, based on their relative strengths and weaknesses – and how these may be connected. For example, a mother who had huge difficulties getting her child to sit at the table and eat his food, but was able at getting him to do his homework, was paired with another parent who managed her children so that they were well behaved during lunch, but found it impossible to motivate them to do their homework. One parent is then placed behind a one-way screen with a member of staff. This parent can hear and see what goes on in the other room and can observe the other parent's struggles. Equipped with a microphone connected to the earpiece worn by the struggling parent, the parent behind the one-way screen makes observations and suggestions as to how the parent interacting with their difficult child could manage him differently. The therapist who sits with the parent behind the one-way screen aims to get her to reflect in this observer position: 'What do you see happening between the mother and her son? Is she being effective right now? What might you do at this stage? How could you put this into words so that the mother can use your ideas? Why don't you try?' Once she has made her 'intervention', the therapist will help her to observe and reflect on the effects. We have found that many parents do have the potential to be a 'supernanny' and a helpful expert – even if they continue to struggle with their own children. Children usually notice that their parent has a 'little man' (or woman) in their ear and they can be asked afterwards what they noticed, above all what the parent did differently. Supernanny sessions should last no longer than 15 minutes as otherwise the person struggling with their child may feel like a remote-controlled robot – and then switch off. The roles then get changed and the supervisor becomes the supervisee. Afterwards parents exchange their own ideas and consider how to implement the 'lessons' learned in their ordinary lives. This exercise helps many parents to believe again in their inner resources, makes them feel proud to be able to help others and increases their feelings of self-worth.

The FDU provides intensive 12-week MFT programmes each year (May–July; September–November; January–March) and up to eight families can attend on any given day, six hours per day, or occasionally longer (up to eight hours). In addition to these block programmes, families can also attend for whole days by themselves or with a few selected families. In other words, the programme is tailor-made for each individual family rather than everyone getting the same input. Consequently some families may attend for ten days over six weeks, others for 25 days over three months, and yet others for perhaps only six days, spaced out over eight weeks. This means that over a 12-week 'module' the FDU can deal with an average of 12 different families. The group is half-open, in the sense that it is a limited group of families, but some families attend on all days – and others only on some. This working environment is in strong contrast to how things were some 20 or 30 years ago when families attended for a whole year and longer. Whilst group membership was then remarkably stable, the work atmosphere was often stagnant. In the current work context, families and staff need to continuously adapt to new group membership, to people coming and going – almost like in real life.

'Therapeutic assessments' of multiproblem families

Many of the families referred to the FDU are involved in court proceedings, with their children either having been removed because of neglect or abuse, or with there being a question as to whether the children should be separated from their families because they are considered to be at risk. In these circumstances the court requests 'parenting assessments' or 'family assessments' and these are commissioned by social services and other similar agencies, so as to assist the court in its decision making. A major aim of these assessments is to examine the past, present and likely future risks of emotional, physical and sexual harm to a child and to provide opinions and make recommendations as to how the child's best interests can be safeguarded in the short and long term. The assessments are child-focused but also take into consideration other significant persons and wider system dimensions: the parents, the extended family, the social and cultural setting, the professional network and other dimensions. The assessment format that the FDU has developed does not merely consist of taking a static snapshot 'photograph' of the current risks and interactions of the family and its individual members, but is a dynamic and interactional process; it could be compared with a 'movie' made by the assessing professionals and the family together. The term 'movie' implies movement – and it is the ability to 'move' – to change – that is crucial when assessing a family and making recommendations about a child's permanent placement and contact levels (Asen and Schuff 2003). Any such changes need to address 'at risk' areas of family functioning and this will take time, usually a few months. Change tends to be a rather slow process, particularly with multiproblem families who have been entrenched in chronic problematic relationship patterns. However, children cannot be expected to wait 'for ever' for their parents to make the required changes. Timescale issues with regard to children's permanency planning have to be kept in mind and hence these 'therapeutic assessments' (Asen 2007c) tend to take some three months on average. Whereas permanent changes are unlikely to be made by the parents and families in such a relatively short time, predictions can nevertheless be made about their potential for change. The focus on the parents' *ability* to change helps to answer some of the important questions with regard to prognosis and likely outcome.

Prior to undertaking the actual work with multiproblem families, we convene a 'network meeting' which has to be attended by all the concerned parties. This includes the parents (or carers), their own 'network', as well as the various professionals involved. It is in this meeting that the focus of the work is defined, with specific questions that need to be addressed. When families attend the FDU, we not only make observations but also immediately feed these back to the parents, highlighting positives and areas of competence, as well as 'negatives' – areas of concern – so that the parents can respond and consider making some of the required changes. This allows us to assess how the parents – and other family members – make use of feedback and whether and how they are able and willing to change. Since it is frequently unrealistic to expect parents to make spontaneous change themselves, particularly if they are stuck in chronic patterns of poor parenting, we need to consider providing supportive interventions, such as straight advice, 'parental coaching', counselling or some other form of more directive family work. Risk needs to be reassessed subsequently, 'post-intervention' as it were, to determine whether it has remained the same, or has been increased or decreased.

We have to keep in mind that parental behaviours, as well as children's, are context dependent. Our team therefore makes many attempts to see parents in a variety of different contexts, not only in the clinic or consulting room, but also in the family home, in school or nursery when picking up their child, on hospital wards, in supermarkets where families often have 'public' crises with their 'unruly' children – and in other settings which are relevant to the family, be that their mosque, church, temple or synagogue. This 'wide-angle' lens approach, if combined with the 'close-up' look at the individual parent and child, permits us to assess the wider context of the family and its support system – and how they can assist and support the family. It is a major principle of therapeutic assessments to work with children and their carers in 'familiar' situations, such as in their home around mealtimes, when picking the children up from school or during a shopping trip. Time and resource issues often do not permit intensive home- and community-based work for individual families. It is for this reason that multi-family day units can be considered as a pragmatic and economic context for intensive therapeutic assessments. Here it is possible to assess the practical parenting ability of a mother or father, in a kind of 'home away from home'. It allows us to see the family in action: how the parents deal with the demands of everyday life; how they organize themselves and their children; how they make decisions and implement these; how they manage under stress; how they prepare meals; how they supervise the children; how they address physical safety issues; how they play; how they plan outings – and so on. A 'typical day in the life of the family' can be re-created in a multi-family setting so that naturalistic interactions can evolve. With other families present, the parents tend to feel less 'centre stage' and the 'spotlight' is not merely on them, but on others as well.

Furthermore, multi-family settings also promote interactions between families. This allows assessing the parents' ability to make social contacts and form relationships, as well as assessing their capacity to supervise their children appropriately when meeting relative 'strangers'. Boundary issues are likely to emerge in a large group of families and can be quite a stressful experience, with all the noise and activity of 15 children and 12 adults. Such levels of stress and intensity are not unwelcome as it requires parents to manage their often volatile emotions in difficult circumstances. This makes it much more difficult for parents who are well practised in putting up a front, or presenting a 'normal' façade, for the sake of professionals. It is also a context in which parents and families can support each other, where they bring their own observations of other families and receive feedback about their problematic or disturbed interactions from other families. Often parents see mirrored in other families precisely those issues that they find difficult to acknowledge themselves.

This model of therapeutic assessments has also been used in other European countries and been adapted to a whole range of different social and legal contexts in France, Belgium, Denmark and Italy, to name but a few (Asen and Bianchi 2007).

Steps into parenthood

A less intensive variation of the FDU work is an MFT group that targets young parents of young children, at-risk families which have not (yet) reached the threshold for social services to become formally involved. Many of the families have the characteristics of multiproblem families – but they seem to manage, just about. They tend to have conflictual relationships with their families of origin, poor social support networks, complex migration histories, unemployment and social marginalization. They are mostly single parents, mothers who may have partners but who do not feel responsible for the children. MFT takes place on a weekly basis in an open group, around lunchtime – from 13.00–14.30 on a Friday – and it is convened by two therapists. Families can attend as much – or as little – as they wish. Some do so only a few times but the majority come fairly regularly and often over the period of a whole year or longer. This can mean that on some Fridays there will be three families and on others ten. The presenting issues tend to be around the typical issues that babies and toddlers present: crying, feeding, temper tantrums, discipline, biting and kicking, jealousy. At the beginning of each session the families and therapists decide on one theme.

A typical example of how the sessions are structured is as follows. The theme for the day, suggested by three parents, is to talk about crying babies and screaming toddlers. Staff may show a brief DVD clip depicting a crying child, possibly selected from a recent episode of a well-known soap opera or other television series which may be familiar to quite a few of the parents who can often identify with the main protagonists. After viewing this clip the therapists may ask:

> 'You all see this screaming baby . . . and probably you have your own ideas why she cried so much and so loud. Let us get away from this case and think about other screaming babies and toddlers and think about all the different reasons why they may cry . . . Please form three groups, with three parents/families each and form little working parties to work out all the reasons why babies cry . . . write these down and in ten minutes the groups can compare notes.'

Once this task is completed – and a record has been to identify 15 reasons for why babies cry – parents are invited to consider what they might do for each form of crying – whether and how to stop it. It is almost inevitable that during the course of the MFT one or more children will cry and this allows parents to test their theories in vivo and speculate on why that baby is crying at that particular point – and what, if anything, should be done about it, with parents providing useful ideas for one another. Whilst discussion themes are initially very concrete and focused on specific difficulties with children, over time other dialogues do also develop. These include domestic violence, alcohol and substance misuse, friendships and whom you can trust, poverty and how to make ends meet, problems with one's own parents and in-laws, etc. Families develop friendships with each other and meet outside the MFT setting. They also bring new families to the group, people they have met in their neighbourhood whom they perceive to be struggling. Slowly a social network develops which becomes a major source of long-term support. Similar projects also take place in other settings and in other countries (El Farricha 2006).

ADHD, Asperger syndrome and other child psychiatric diagnoses

No matter what one may think about the 'reality' or scientific evidence base of specific child psychiatric disorders, it is a fact that diagnoses like attention deficit hyperactivity disorder (ADHD), Asperger syndrome and Tourette's syndrome are becoming increasingly – and worryingly – more popular each year. Increasingly teachers and parents want to hear from child psychiatrists and psychologists that their child's worrying behaviour is a 'real' illness or disorder, and they can be very disappointed if, for example, a diagnosis of ADHD is not made. Having access to child and adolescent mental health services which are not adverse to making such diagnoses but still employ a systemic framework is often a way forward. One such example is the Familientagesklinik (Family Day Clinic, FDC) based at the University Hospital Dresden (Universitätsklinikum Carl Gustav Carus) which was opened more than ten years ago (Scholz *et al.* 2002). Each year some 65 families are treated here, with the main target group being children between the ages of 3 and 13 who have been diagnosed with one of the above-mentioned child psychiatric disorders. The child has to attend the FDC accompanied by at least one parent (or other carer). Other family members, such as grandparents, siblings or aunts, participate some of the time. The Dresden team has found that approximately half of the parents attending also present with a diagnosed – or diagnosable – mental health issue. Families come from very different social strata and a significant number of parents are unemployed. The number of families seen at the same time is on average five. Prior to being accepted for FDC attendance, there are a number of outpatient assessments to make a diagnosis and look at the indication for this form of work. Parents are told about the purpose and structure of the FDC and given plenty of time to decide whether or not they wish to attend. There is no pressure from social services or other services and all families attend entirely on a voluntary basis, quite different from the majority of the families attending the London FDU – they feel coerced and are initially very reluctant to work on themselves. This is quite different in Dresden and reflects a predominantly medical setting and a clientele which has been diagnosed with a specific illness or disorder.

In Dresden MFT takes place in a day setting, just as in London, and as all children live with their parents – unlike the clientele attending the London FDU – the families return home after their day. Therapy is intensive and brief, lasting on average four to six weeks. The aim of therapy is not to solve specific problems once and for all, but to enable families, after a short sharp burst of input, to continue the work subsequently with only outpatient support – usually in the form of single family therapy, parental counselling and also at times individual work with a child or parent. Much emphasis is placed on working with the family's social network and the helping system. Work involves primary and nursery schools, as well as home visits. The group is 'half-open', with new families joining when others leave. The team is particularly keen to make even small changes visible and celebrate these. It is interesting to note that a short time after the FDC was opened, the children's inpatient ward could be closed – a first in a German university hospital setting where the number of inpatient beds signals the power of the chief doctor.

Each day has a clear structure, pre-given by staff but negotiable. Each family is asked to find ways of using the structure for their specific purposes. On Wednesdays families create the structure and timetable themselves (see Table 6.3).

Table 6.3 Family day clinic: weekly timetable

Time	Monday	Tuesday	Wednesday	Thursday	Friday
7:45					
8:00	Breakfast	Breakfast		Breakfast	Breakfast
8:15					
			Children in mainstream school	Children in clinic school	Children in clinic school
8:30	Children in clinic school	Children in clinic school			
8:45					
9:00				Parents in planning meeting	Parents in planning meeting
9:15	Parents in planning meeting	Parents in planning meeting		Video feedback	Video feedback
		Video feedback			
	Individual work with parents				
9:30		Once fortnightly parents' group			
9:45					
10:00				Single family sessions	
10:15		Single family sessions	Home visits		MFT activity
10:30	MFT activity			MFT activity	
10:45		MFT activity	or		
11:00			Single family sessions/ parental couple work		
11:15		Movement/ exercise/ relaxation group			
11:30				Parallel parents' and children's groups	
11:45	Movement/ exercise/ relaxation group				
12:00					
12:15					

Table 6.3 Continued

Time	Monday	Tuesday	Wednesday	Thursday	Friday
12:30	Lunch break	Lunch break		Lunch break	Lunch break
12:45					
13:00					
13:15	Sessions/ home work/ Art therapy	Sessions/ homework/ Art therapy			Reflective group
13:30					
13:45					
14:00	Free time/ homework	Free time/ homework		outing	
14:15					Coffee break/ teatime
14:30	Flashlight	Flashlight			
14:45					
15:00	Coffee break/ teatime	Coffee break/ teatime			
15:15					
15:30			Flashlight	Flashlight	

Another family day clinic in a child and adolescent psychiatry department setting has been in place for some 15 years now, at the University of Münster in Germany. It specializes in the early recognition of and intervention in attachment disorders and other forms of relationship disturbances in pre-school children.

Similar work is carried out at the Marlborough Family Service, often in combination with single family therapy and parental couple work. For some years now the London team has also provided inputs to other child and adolescent mental health services in the South East of England, including for children and adolescents who have been diagnosed with Asperger syndrome. Here we put together up to eight families with diagnosed children, together with their respective families, including siblings. A programme that has proved successful consists of ten sessions, each lasting two and a half hours, at fortnightly intervals, starting at 16.30. When families arrive they find some (good quality) snacks and (non-alcoholic) drinks displayed on a large table and they tend to congregate here initially. It is often surprising to see how quickly some children with the diagnosis of Asperger syndrome mix with other children and how quickly contacts between allegedly 'communication-disabled' families are being made.

After this informal encounter, families are seated in rows facing a podium. The therapy team can preside over the next segment of the session, but instead of providing formal psycho-education for the families, find out what the families know themselves. This can be done by asking simple questions such as:

> 'Who in this room knows something about what Asperger syndrome is? Please do not all talk at once, but put up your hands and we will hear from each person in turn . . . We will first want to hear what the children and teenagers know . . . So how can we tell that a person has Asperger's? What are the symptoms? How does it affect other family members?'

A flipchart can be used and a member of staff can note down the points that are being made. It is our experience that if one pools the knowledge of all the different families and their individual members, there is very little expert knowledge which staff need to supplement. This can be followed by convening a 'press conference', asking one or two of the children to take their place on the podium and giving a formal introduction to 'Living with Mr Asperger'. MFT activities and exercises that are particularly suited to working with this group of families are 'frozen statues', 'feeling games', 'mind-brain scans'. 'Guess what's wrong with me' is a related exercise, involving all the children, including siblings, with the parents placed in an outside observer position. Children are asked by way of questioning what the feeling states of a particular person are. A member of staff can act as 'the patient', presenting initially with low mood, later with anger, or being anxious. The children are asked to be the doctors who need to examine the patient and then decide on a suitable treatment. Later the parents reflect on what they have observed and this usually brings out themes of 'ability to empathize' – something most children with the diagnosis of Asperger's seem to be able to do when in play. In later groups one can look at specific behaviours that the parents complain about in their diagnosed child and then think about whether other explanations might also be equally plausible. One can take up issues such as 'not wanting to listen' as opposed to 'simply not being able to take it in', or to look at which challenging behaviours are signs of the disorder and which are merely 'naughty'. In this way the presentation of specific seemingly disorder-related symptoms become deconstructed.

Chapter 7

Working with and in schools

This chapter introduces a multilayered model of intervening with problem pupils, their families and the larger school system. The therapeutic work takes place in an education-based multi-family context, with families providing peer support as well as challenging one another. This unique approach was pioneered at the Marlborough Family Service and has subsequently been replicated in many different settings in the United Kingdom and in several European countries. The work is carried out both via a 'Family School' and 'Family Classes' – the former being a bespoke off-site unit and the latter being based in mainstream schools. In addition, parallel work with teachers, schools and the wider education system takes place.

Family and school education

Rather than considering a pupil's behaviour in isolation, the systemic approach focuses on context and on the relationships between pupil, school and family (Aponte 1976; Tucker and Dryson 1976; Relph 1984; Dowling and Osborne 1985; Roffey 2002). The aim is to counteract the potential for overemphasizing individual or institutional blame. A family systems perspective is useful at all stages of school life as children are continually affecting, as well as being affected by, the key relationships in their lives. It hardly needs stating that family events and crises are likely to influence a child's ability to function in school. When there is violence in the home which children are powerless to stop, or other forms of chronic states of family tension or crisis, they can become anxious and unfocused and present in school as 'distractable' and 'challenging'. In line with their own experiences of how relationship issues get negotiated, children may themselves become violent in the classroom or school playground. If caught up in parental conflicts, children become familiar with taking sides, often seeking to protect the most vulnerable person, usually their mother. In school this can be re-enacted when teachers who are perceived as being unfair, or as victimizing a pupil, are challenged. Other pupils, because of being preoccupied with matters at home, can present as withdrawn when in class or plainly refuse to go to school.

Some of these children stay at home as they see it as their role to be their mother's 'bodyguard' to prevent domestic violence. A systemic perspective can assist when trying to make sense of a child's difficulties in school (Holmes 1982; Dombalis and Erchul 1987; Rendall and Stewart 2005) and connecting these with their home experiences (Dawson and McHugh 1987).

The approach pioneered by the Marlborough Family Education Centre (MFEC), which is part of the Marlborough Family Service (MFS) in London, aims to bridge the often huge gap between the world of education (school) and the home (family). To many systemic practitioners the term 'family education' may suggest psycho-educational practices, or indeed evoke images of 'nanny state' type of interventions, with experts educating families or parents in classrooms. This is not the approach promoted by the MFEC. Instead it encourages families to learn for themselves and to 'educate' each other, by working together in an education-based multi-family setting. The MFEC delivers its interventions for pupils and their families both on site in mainstream primary and secondary schools ('Family Classes') and via a bespoke unit based at the MFS ('Family School'). In both settings pupils not only benefit from continuing their education by following the ordinary school curriculum, but their parents are centrally involved in assisting them to generate more acceptable interactions with other pupils, teachers and parents. This approach also addresses antisocial behaviour and increases academic success at school by escaping the vicious cycle of problem behaviours, poor academic achievement and social exclusion.

The Family School

The establishment of the Family School (Dawson and McHugh 1986), jointly funded by health and education services, more than two decades ago was prompted by an increasing number of referrals of pupils who had been excluded from their mainstream schools because of disruptive classroom behaviours, violence and/or serious 'learning blocks'. The referring teachers tended to put all the blame for the pupil's problems at the family's door, whereas the family blamed the school entirely for the problem behaviours and educational failure of their child(ren), citing poor teaching, lack of discipline or inadequate supervision of their child at school. The resulting impasse placed the pupil increasingly in the middle between the warring parties, with the teachers asking the parents to seek expert psychological help and the parents refusing to do so, requesting instead that the schools get 'their act together'. Even the threat of permanent exclusion would not motivate the parents to accept referrals to the local child and adolescent mental health services, with many parents fearing scrutiny of their parenting skills and possible stigmatization. The concept of 'parental presence' in mainstream schools, permitting parents to witness their child's difficulties in vivo, seemed a way forward but it was not acceptable in the 1980s. By contrast, the newly founded Family School could be attended by the pupil and one or two of the parents or other carers and in this way they could learn first hand about their child in an educational context and see how family issues were at times being re-enacted in school (Dawson and McHugh 1994).

All pupils attending the Family School need to be on the roll of a mainstream school, as the aim is always to reintegrate them once improvements in their behavioural and emotional presentations have taken place. If a child has been permanently excluded, the local education authority is asked to identify a school which the pupil can attend once the required changes have been made. Children for whom there is no school are not accepted, and this tends to intensify the search. The reason for insisting on there being an identified school is to prevent the Family School becoming an 'end of the road' institution and a 'bin' for society's marginalized and unwanted children. When children first attend the Family School, it may well be that they only go to their mainstream school for one hour per week, which at times is all its teachers can manage. However, once children's behaviours improve in the Family School setting, increasingly longer spells in the mainstream school are negotiated. It is not at all uncommon that within three months many pupils will attend the Family School in the mornings and their mainstream school in the afternoon. The majority of pupils will have reduced their Family School attendance to one morning per week after six months, with the rest of their time being spent in their mainstream primary or secondary school, now almost full time. In order for this to succeed, it is essential for there to be a collaborative relationship between professionals working in both settings, with continuous feedback between the institutions.

The Family School is designed to function as a classroom with the normal pupils' desks and attendant educational equipment. In addition, within the classroom, there is a small kitchen area and also a space with comfortable seating for the parents or other adults, placing them in 'observer' positions, as well as permitting them to talk to each other and exchange experiences while their children are engaged in learning activities. The setting is recognizably 'educational', but at the same time also different from an ordinary school. The classroom can accommodate ten pupils, between the ages of five and 16, and their families and this provides them with the possibility of talking about their conflictual relationships with the school system and their children's problematic behaviours both in school and at home. There is a special atmosphere of immediacy and intensity, as issues emerging in one family frequently have significant meaning for other families. Parents have often stated that it is more difficult to pretend that changes are taking place in a multi-family group setting. For example, a 14-year-old boy was referred to the Family School for poor school attendance and lack of focus. Teachers complained that he seemed to expect 'special treatment' and had angry outbursts if he was not responded to immediately. In the Family School his mother spoke about how she had insisted that her son should deliver newspapers in the mornings and learn to budget with the money he earned. Whilst staff were impressed by this mother's seeming resolve to no longer 'baby' her son and get him to become more responsible, another mother in the group then questioned this account by asking the boy why she had seen his mother repeatedly delivering 'his' newspapers. This challenge led to a useful discussion, involving all members of the multi-family group, about how parents cover – and 'cover up' – for their offspring. When people are not changing, the rest of the group want to know why not and ask about what needs to happen for something to shift. There is group pressure, for example when a father reports back that he was unable to implement some specific consequences the previous night. He is likely to be challenged by other parents – and often also by children from other families. This dynamic can lead to spirited exchanges which are not readily available in the more traditional professional/client relationships. It is far harder to ignore feedback from somebody who has first-hand knowledge of a similar predicament than from a clinician who may be seen as only having learned about these issues 'by proxy' or from textbooks.

The Family School is staffed by three professionals with dual qualifications: they are teachers and they have received systemic trainings, reflecting their parallel tasks of teacher and therapist. This double stance makes it possible to observe and address the difficulties that pupils have in their relationship to the curriculum set, their interactions with the teacher and peers, as well as in intra-family relationships. The task for staff is to convert teacher observations into issues that carry relational meaning and to use these as potential vehicles for change (Carlson 1987). This is very different from the traditional position of teachers, who when confronted with problematic behaviours would expect to have to resolve the situation themselves.

The Family School group is 'open' in the sense that new pupils and their families can join when a place becomes vacant, allowing current service users – 'experts by experience' – to explain the model to newcomers. Pupils initially attend with at least one significant adult/carer together for four mornings each week, for three hours. As it is important for pupils attending the Family School to keep up with the mainstream school curriculum, in order to combat threatening marginalization, close collaboration with the teachers from the mainstream schools is essential. Whilst mainstream schools want to see rapid and lasting changes in their highly problematic pupils, in reality such miracles rarely happen. Hence the Family School involves the pupil's mainstream school as collaborator(s) in a joint project, with mainstream teachers serving as monitors of the effectiveness of the Family School's therapeutic interventions. The marking of daily behavioural targets (see below) provides the 'live' context for evaluating progress, not only of the pupil but also of the mainstream school teachers who themselves can at times be remarkably fixed or 'stuck' in their views of the child. If they cannot 'move on', neither will the pupil be able to. Mainstream school teachers, in turn, can also helpfully challenge the Family School staff's optimism with regard to change or taking sides with the family against a particular teacher. Providing contexts to explore and address these and related issues is essential and counteracts further splitting. Regular meetings involving all participants – pupil, parents, mainstream school teachers and Family School staff – help to make transparent the complex individual and organizational relationships and facilitate open discussion.

The daily Family School programme has two main strands: education and therapeutic intervention. Families arrive from 9.00 am onwards and tend to have breakfast together and talk informally, about everyday issues or about their successes and failures with their child and family. This helps to build up contacts between families which can then be continued after school, in the evenings and during weekends. It is not uncommon for families to exchange their mobile phone numbers and visit each other's homes once they have got to know each other. This can help to overcome social isolation and increases children's and parents' self-confidence and social competence. The first formal part of a morning session, from 9.30 to 9.45, is the planning meeting when parents and children together identify the goals for each family for that day. Plans are made as to how 'old' behaviours can be challenged and 'new' relationships can be developed. At the end of this meeting each pupil has identified a goal and knows who is 'on their team' to help defeat old troubling habits and promote new potentially more successful ways of being. Parents may also elect to have challenges and goals for the day. Following this meeting, children are taught formally in the classroom and their parents can also sometimes sit with their child and assist them with their specific scholastic task. with their parents or other family members observing from the sidelines. However, parents mostly observe the action from the sidelines, sitting in a semi-circle away from the school desks. At times they can act as a 'Greek chorus' or a reflecting team, commenting on what they observe and occasionally springing into action. For example, a father who observes his son being repeatedly rude to a teacher may get up, walk over to his son and admonish him. A mother may defend her daughter against the seemingly unfair accusations of the teacher. This can lead to heated discussions, with other parents and pupils becoming involved and providing their own views. The role of Family School staff is to encourage parent and child, with the help of other families, to address and resolve problematic issues 'here and now'. It is a common experience that precisely those problems that have led to the pupil's exclusion get quickly re-enacted in the setting of the Family School. This includes kicking other pupils under the table, being verbally or physically aggressive towards a teacher, refusing to complete a specific piece of schoolwork. Since the parents are always present in the classroom and not far away from the action, they become experts in spotting pupils' problem behaviours. They can discuss with other parents whether or not they should get involved in disciplining their own child in the Family School or whether this should be left to the teacher.

After the first lesson all pupils and family members join a structured meeting (at 10.15 am) which lasts 50 minutes. The meeting is chaired by one of the Family School staff or a parent, with one other group member, a child or parent, acting as co-chair and timekeeper. Each family has their own five-minute slot which is divided into three parts. The family can use the first two minutes as they wish, but usually to report back to the group on how the last 24 hours have gone in relation to their specific goals for change. These goals are clearly defined behavioural targets, both for the school and the home setting, and are rated on a daily basis by teachers and parents. During the first two minutes, it is the chair's responsibility to ensure that the members of a specific family report back to the group. For the second two-minute slot, the chair and co-chair work together to manage the flow of information around the group, inviting other members of the multi-family group to make observations and comments about what has just been said; about any changes that they might have noticed; about an observation of how the child or parent has been trying something different; or about how the family members seem to be 'getting stuck'. The group gives applause for family members meeting their goals. In the remaining one minute the behavioural targets are reviewed and specific emerging themes may be used to set the next target(s). In this meeting it is the timekeeper's sole task to let everybody know when it is time to move on to the next family. Teachers from the pupil's mainstream schools are invited to attend this meeting and to witness this ritual.

It is evident that not everything can be covered in only five minutes per family. However, there are several interesting consequences of maintaining such tight time boundaries. They help to reduce the amount of redundant information, or 'cracked records' as they are often referred to, and encourage family members to focus on how they are going to use their time. Leaving a 'hot' family issue at the end of the allocated five minutes without a neat resolution invariably provokes charged discussions between the families after the formal meeting has ended, with Family School staff then taking a 'back seat' and allowing the group of families to find their own resolutions. At the end of this meeting usually each family has been given several ideas by the group and they are encouraged to take these back to school and home and try them out. Families are explicitly asked to report back the next day on which ideas worked for them. There is an expectation by the group of families that such homework will be completed and this acts as a considerable motivating pressure.

This meeting is followed by a break, with pupils and their parents spending a few minutes in the playground, often to 'let off steam'. Break time is a typical context in which specific problematic interactions can occur and 'parental presence' (Omer 2004) in the playground is essential so that parents take responsibility for children whilst Family School staff meet to plan the next phase of the morning's programme. The last part of the morning is often based on issues or themes that have emerged during the morning. There is the possibility of a range of activities and exercises, including formal teaching and lessons, with parents then implementing strategies they identified earlier. For example, a 'distant' father may decide to sit next to his son who struggles with maths, experiencing the child's distress from a position of close proximity. Another parent who has come to recognize that she is too closely involved with her son may experiment with different ways of creating distance and space. Children may try out different ways of asking for help and their parents may be helped to practise 'not responding', or responding differently, to provocative or attention-seeking behaviours. Parents are also frequently encouraged to interact temporarily with children from other families and 'foster' them for an hour or so. Here the parent who is observing their child with another adult has a chance to see how things can be different. Similarly, the child who is observing their parent relating to another child is given a view of how there could be different possibilities for their own relationship. The Family School has also set up literacy classes for parents, with the help of colleagues working in adult education. Here parents learn to improve their literacy skills, with the help of laptops, and this parallel learning context not only boosts parents' competence with new technologies and enhances their self-confidence, but also sends a message about the importance of learning to their own children.

Behavioural targets and consequences

At the very outset of the work in the Family School there is a deliberate focus on those problem behaviours which have led to the pupil's exclusion or threat of exclusion. Problematic behaviours that teachers list include poor concentration span, 'hyperactivity', disruptiveness, poor literacy and numerical skills, non-compliance, lack of motivation, poor behavioural and social skills, low self-image and lack of confidence, tearing up schoolwork, problematic peer relationships, poor anger management and other self-control issues. In a first meeting with the school and the family, all involved are asked to pinpoint specific behaviours of the child that they feel are problematic. Children are encouraged to say what they need from the adults present at the meeting if they are to change their behaviours. A common request from children is for their parents to stop arguing and for teachers to be more attentive to their classroom and playground needs. Precise and concrete behavioural goals for the pupil are then jointly agreed, for the classroom, other areas of school and sometimes also for the home. Children are marked for each behavioural target on a scale from 1 to 4, with 4 being the top score for consistently meeting the specific target. Both the Family School and mainstream teachers are asked to note comments regarding the targets, and the parents are requested to check the scores each day and to clarify with the teacher(s) any trouble that the child might have had. In this way a daily feedback loop is established between family and school. Children's scores are discussed on a daily basis during the meeting described above. Once a child consistently obtains good scores on one target, a new target will be set. The consistent improvement in a child's score on behavioural targets is a clear indicator that change has taken place. The child becomes more able to understand what needs to change, going beyond the often all too general request of having to be a 'good child'. Improvement in behavioural targets is met with specific rewards that have been previously agreed upon by the family, as well as receiving praise from the assembled multi-family group each time positive marks are reported. The behavioural targets also act as a tool for the family, namely to develop clearer hierarchies and boundaries within the family, as well as establishing explicit and consistent relationships between target behaviours and resulting consequences. Furthermore, when children begin to consistently receive positive marks, it becomes easier to change their negative reputation at school. The fact that the teacher has specific behaviours to concentrate on makes it easier to notice changes: too often the general focus on 'bad behaviour' dominates over positive changes a pupil may make in specific areas. Behavioural targets thus become a tangible document of a pupil's improvement. The targets are deliberately very concrete and can be easily observed and scored (see Table 7.1). Initially, the targets are all focused on the child's behaviour at school, but most parents opt sooner rather than later for doing the same at home. As a result specific home targets get drawn up with child and parent, to do with eating, going to bed, playing with the computer. Children sometimes set targets for their parents, like not shouting at them, to be home when the

Table 7.1 M's school targets

Has M?		
Kept his hands and feet to himself	❏4❏3❏2❏1	
	All of the time	Not at all
Done as he was told first time	❏4❏3❏2❏1	
	All of the time	Not at all
Listened to what the lunchtime supervisors have told him to do and asked them to help if he has a problem	❏4❏3❏2❏1	
	All of the time	Not at all
Completed a written piece of work	❏4❏3❏2❏1	
	Very well	Not at all
Shared well with other children	❏4❏3❏2❏1	
	All of the time	Not at all
Spoken respectfully to Mum	❏4❏3❏2❏1	
	All of the time	Not at all
Signed..Date..	M T W T F	

child returns from school, and so on. The discussion around the targets helps to shape the therapeutic agenda for each family.

Parents like to have information from school on a daily basis rather than living in dread of the phone call that comes when behaviours have escalated to a critical stage. The evolving feedback loops and continuing discussions about change between the family and the school are one of the benefits of the target system. Confronted by low scores, parents have a chance to discuss what is going wrong and to talk about difficulties they may have in, for example, setting limits or focusing on strengths. At this point it is common for parents to talk in the group about their own personal traumata or childhood difficulties and how these may adversely affect their parenting. The parents have the opportunity to discuss this in a 'parents only' group without their children being present. A considerable number of parents who have resisted previous offers of individual help for themselves recognize the impact of their own unresolved issues on their children and will ask for individual thera-peutic help or parental couple work to address emotional and mental health issues. This can be provided by members of the multidisciplinary team of the Marlborough Family Service.

When it comes to discussing the consequences of meeting – or not meet-ing – the targets, it is important to involve parents and children together. Children often have clearer ideas than their parents about rewards and pun-ishments – the latter mostly taking the form of withdrawal of privileges. Initially, children can be motivated by short-term, concrete consequences and material rewards. However, surprisingly often they express pleasure at more relational rewards such as: 'I like it when my Mum looks happy and my teachers smile at me.' In the multi-family group, families also share ideas and make helpful suggestions. This open discussion creates group pressure in that it leads to follow-up questions when, for example, parents ask one individual mother whether she was able to implement the consequences she had deci-ded upon during the previous evening. Quite a number of parents have 'confessed' that the only reason why they carried out the consequences was because they could not face the group the next day if they had not. Consequences plans (Table 7.2) are written and displayed prominently in the family home, so that everybody can remember them.

Behavioural targets are popular not only with parents but also with main-stream school teachers as they enable them to measure a pupil's progress concretely, particularly if the data are collected on a weekly basis over a period of time. Progressively good results can convince even the most sceptical teacher to consider that a previously 'impossible' pupil spends increasingly more time in their school.

Other techniques employed in education-based multi-family work include *sand-timers* (five minutes or ten minutes). They encourage children with poor concentration to 'beat your own record' with regard to the length of time during which they can focus on schoolwork without interrupting others

Table 7.2 J's Consequences plan

---

1 If you get any 1s in a day and get into a mood about it:
   Consequence – you are grounded in your room after the Marlborough for three days in a row.

2 If you get any 2s in a day and you get into a mood about it:
   Consequence – you are grounded in your room for the rest of the day.

3 If you get any 1s or 2s in a day but you stay out of a mood:
   Consequence – you are grounded in the flat for the rest of the day.

4 If you get all 3s and 4s in a day:
   Consequence – you will get praised and you will be allowed out.

---

or being interrupted. *Traffic lights* can be helpful for children with a reputation for being 'highly volatile'. Red, green and amber flashcards act as an early visual warning system for the child. The amber card, shown to the child by a parent or teacher, warns that the child is starting to get restless or challenging. If the child manages to contain his explosive state(s), a green card is shown and praise given. If the child continues the escalation, a further visual reminder to change track is given, before finally the red card is shown – for many boys only too reminiscent of what happens on the football pitch for bad behaviour. The showing of amber or red cards frequently slows down or interrupts the cycle of mutual escalation and has proved a useful technique that can also be employed in the family home. *Well done cards* aim to counteract many children's absent experience of ever having received certificates for good behaviour or educational achievement in their mainstream schools. Certificates to emphasize change and help parents to notice new behaviours are given during the morning in the Family School and children are encouraged to take these to their mainstream school in the afternoon to help with the process of changing their reputations. A prominently displayed *rewards box* invites parents to contribute ideas for how to reward children. This helps parents to build up resources and new routines and to challenge current parenting practices, from overly generous giving, appeasing or actual bribing, to having very high parental expectations which are impossible for children to meet. *Certificates* are also issued to parents by other parents, to children by parents and by children to parents. In the Family School each family has a noticeboard where evidence of change can be prominently displayed, be that certificates, photographs, drawings or high scores the children receive at home, in the Family School and in the mainstream school. A little booklet, entitled *Staircase to Success*, is filled in daily with an agreed family reward at the top. This is a popular visual reminder that change is not just designed or needed for one day. Celebration can occur when a child has coloured in a number of steps towards the agreed reward. This could be, for example, a family picnic or a trip to the cinema.

From this account it may seem that in the Family School plenty of seemingly 'linear' behavioural techniques are used to promote change. Furthermore, the emphasis on achieving targets could be seen as unhelpfully mirroring the current politically driven preoccupation, if not obsession, with achieving measurable change, however banal, which has invaded the education system and other settings. In our view the behavioural targets and related consequences provide a helpful initial focus for concretely monitoring and measuring progress. They also create useful contexts for focusing on specific family interactions, as well as increasing family–school interactions. The goal is not to turn children into some human rats who are conditioned in specific ways so as to get their cheese or other reward at the end of the maze. The initial aim is to change problematic behaviours first so that the children can be viewed – and to view themselves – differently. However, the mere marking of behavioural targets by allegedly 'neutral observers', i.e. teachers or parents, is not sufficient to promote deeper and lasting change. We encourage pupils to mark themselves, as well as imagining how their teachers or parents might mark – or have marked – them on each target. Parents can also rate the child's behaviour in the classroom and imagine how the child might want to rate it. In this way real and imagined multiratings are generated. These can then be compared and discussions can ensue as to why different people have come with different results. In the classroom other pupils can be asked to guess what marks pupils gave – and should give – to themselves and to provide their own marks. If different teachers give different marks for the same child on the same targets, all families can speculate what this may be about. Discussing discrepancies and putting oneself into the heads and shoes of others helps to generate and respect multiple perspectives. The major endeavour is for families and their individual members to reflect on the significance of how they interact around targets and consequences; to question their own actions; to tune into their related feelings and those of others; and to challenge their own and each other's beliefs.

As the Family School is a day setting, there is plenty of opportunity to have brief ad hoc single family sessions, consultations with individual family members or parental couple mini-sessions. These take place outside the multi-family group setting, in a side room, in the corridor, or in the garden. In the 'pressure cooker' of the Family School, it is very common for strong emotional experiences or traumatic memories to 'bubble up' in a child or parent, usually in direct response to concrete experiences in the classroom, in response to not meeting a specific target or implementing consequences, or receiving a 'red card'. Having the opportunity of immediate ad hoc sessions with staff, be these individual, couple or family meetings, is experienced by many as being more useful than having to 'save' their distress for a (traditional) 50-minute session some days or weeks later.

In the early years it seemed that going to the families' homes was the best way of engaging seemingly 'resistant' parents, to allay their fears and to convince them to accept the referral. Over recent years the team has largely stopped undertaking such home visits and come to rely on members of the multi-family group to engage new families thinking about taking up a place at the Family School (Dawson and McHugh 2000). The prospective family is invited to visit the Family School just to look at what goes on there, without any expectation of a commitment to take up a place at this stage. After a brief discussion with the child and their parents, they are introduced to one or more of the parents who are already attending the Family School with their own child. They are left alone together and are advised to find out as much as they can about what actually happens and whether the place can be of any use or not. Since social isolation and feelings of hopelessness are general features of families referred to the MFEC, this first encounter with a family which has been in the same position before attending the Family School, and which has experienced some change for the better, is an excellent way of giving a new family some hope that things can get better.

Family Classes

Over the years we have realized that many of the pupils referred to the MFEC arrive at a rather late stage and often some time after they had been excluded from their mainstream school. This led the team to consider a series of out-reach projects in different primary and secondary schools and the 'Family Class' concept was born (Dawson and McHugh 2005). Negotiations took place with various head teachers and there was a general consensus that school-based MFT, once a week for two or three hours, during ordinary school hours would be viable. Teachers at the local schools identify pupils and invite their parents to attend a Family Class. This is run jointly by a 'graduate' parent – a mother or father who has successfully attended the Family School with their offspring; a school-based partner (teacher, learn-ing assistant or special needs coordinator) and a member of the MFEC team, named 'early intervention worker'. 'Graduate' pupils (previous Family School or Family Class attenders) mentor or 'buddy' other children on these outreach programmes. Six to eight families attend the Family Class once weekly, usually for one term, and the structure is similar to what is on offer in the Family School, with an initial emphasis on targets and consequences, as well as time for reflection, discussion, playfulness, and so on. These groups necessarily operate at a lower level of intensity than the Family School, as the children's difficulties generally are not at the same crisis level and the parents have not usually got to the same level of desperation. However, the children are those whom the teachers have identified as causing significant problems in school and who would be likely to become increasingly worrying if specific help was not found for them. By attending the Family Classes, parents are not required to 'sign up' for any formal therapy but to commit themselves to trying to help their children to be more successful in school. The intervention is focused on helping children to change behaviours, but with the understanding that this should lead to more successful functioning in school and likely to be associated with improved academic performance. The school-based partner is central in helping to embed the potential changes emanating from the multi-family group work into the wider school context. Feedback when something is going well can be almost immediate, with other teachers from the school being welcome to participate in sessions as appropriate and when they can be released from their other responsibilities. Similarly, when things are not going so well, it is possible to get the key people involved together at short notice to consider what happened and to work together with the individual and the other group members to find more successful solutions. The discussions and planning pre- and post-groups give an opportunity for skills and knowledge exchanges between the partners who come from very different professional backgrounds. The early intervention worker has to learn very quickly how to adapt to the school setting in terms of the routines and structures and to be mindful of what is and is not possible to do in someone else's domain. The school-based partner is offered the chance to learn a probably new systemic way of thinking about a child's problems in school and to join in with constructing interventions that can be relevant in the school setting. We have found that the quality of this partnership is the bedrock on which successful Family Classes in school can be built. If the school partner has a 'systemic inclination', as many good teachers do, and is also in a position of some authority within the school such that they can influence their colleagues' thinking and practice, then the Family Classes are highly successful (Dawson and McHugh 2006).

The 'graduate' parents, referred to as 'parent-partners', who co-run the groups are excellent at helping anxious or sceptical parents to join and participate in the family classroom with the professionals. As 'living proof' that this multi-family group approach has worked for them, they can be very convincing when describing their own experiences of former struggles and what helped them to overcome many of their difficulties. The parent-partners are invariably very good at 'recruiting' worrying children and their parents who they know about through their own informal parent and playground communication network. By offering their expertise from their own experiences, parent-partners generally gain in self-esteem through their leading role in the Family Classes. Many parents who have taken on this role have gone on to train in their own right to work in this or associated fields – an outcome that most would have never considered possible when they themselves were going through serious difficulties with their children, or when schools had 'excluded' the parents from the school premises because of their challenging and aggressive behaviours. One of the 'graduate' parents said about herself:

> 'I used to be the teachers' worst nightmare. I was always at the school complaining that my boy was not being treated right by the teachers.

I could never believe that he would do anything wrong, I was always in the head teacher's office demanding that he do something. It was only after I'd been to the Marlborough that I realized where I was going wrong. I used to think that if I told my children off they wouldn't love me so I had to learn to be their Mum and not try to be their friend all the time.'

This mother has recently been employed as a special learning assistant by the very school that had banned her from the premises some four years ago.

It is important not to forget the other classmates and their parents in a child's mainstream class. They may, through previous experience of a child, maintain strong views about a child who is attending the Family School. Their habitual behaviours and beliefs can be strong barriers to change in the main school contexts. We tackle this problem by creating and using a number of new relationships. Children are invited by the class teacher to offer a 'buddy' service to a child attending the Family School. They have the task of helping the identified child stay on track in school and they are assisted in this by the teacher and classroom assistants. If and when the buddy notices positive behavioural or relational change in the classroom or playground and brings this to the attention of the staff or peers, they in turn are rewarded. Parents who have graduated from the Family School can work as assistants in most local schools and tell the 'good news' to other parents in the school. Family School newsletters are published where some children and parents and their teachers tell their stories of success (Omer 2004). Head teachers have frequently reported that they like instituting Family Classes as part of their school's pastoral support repertoire because they act as a good resource for those children and their parents who normally would cause the head teacher the most difficulties. Family Classes can become the place to which head teachers can easily refer anxious parents, in marked contrast to the more complex and often less successful usual referral route to child and adolescent mental health services.

More recently we have experimented with a biofeedback device which is used to 'externalize' internal physiological states (McHugh *et al.*, 2010). Heart rate monitors, emitting audible signals in the form of a bleep when a specific threshold is reached, are fitted to children and members of the family. This can help all those present to make connections between problematic behaviours and internal states of emotional/physical arousal. When parents and their children are 'wired up' with heart rate monitors at the same time, they can explore how they work each other up and how confrontations can escalate. Discussions often arise as to 'who bleeped first' and in an MFT context multiple perspectives and explanations can be offered. Once the bleeping has stopped and some emotional equilibrium has been regained, it is possible to involve the participants in reflecting about their own and others' feelings states and how the whole sequence evolved. Devices can be worn for up to 24 hours and computer graph printouts of fluctuating heart rates can assist in contextualizing problematic interactions, particularly if other family members are also fitted with heart rate monitors. In this way biofeedback becomes 'systemic' as people become alerted to the interconnectedness of each other's feeling states and emotional arousal. However, participants are not only helped to identify stressors leading to heightened states of emotional arousal and resulting 'out of control' behaviours, but also to find ways of employing (self-)calming strategies. With the help of these biofeedback devices pupils – and their parents – begin to manage themselves in situations which previously would have resulted in stressed, angry or violent behaviours. Whilst individuals vary markedly in the time it takes to regain composure after arousal, it is striking to observe that many children have similar patterns of recovery to their parents. Apart from actual situations of conflict it is also possible to help children and parents to imagine problematic situations or hypothetical scenarios as a means of 'tuning into' their internal states, with the aid of the monitors. Merely thinking about a highly problematic situation can accelerate the heart rate, and the more families can spot the 'minefields' of their emotional terrain, the easier it is to time the initiation of self-calming strategies. When using these devices during MFT we have observed that people more readily engage with managing their own arousal and emotional responses when they see other adults and children acknowledging and attempting to cope with theirs.

Hearing about the heart monitor feedback work and observing the evidence from the printouts can help teachers and other education professionals to begin to think differently about their problem pupils and their efforts to change. Similarly, when the children's parents open up about their own stress reactions, teachers have often found it a humbling experience and have become less ready to criticize the parents. In this way both the Family School and Family Classes are contexts for continuing education and learning.

Chapter 8

Eating disorders, psychosis and mood disorders

In this chapter we describe the application of MFT to different types of eating disorders – anorexia nervosa, bulimia nervosa and childhood obesity – and other major presentations in the field of adult psychiatry, namely psychosis and mood disorders.

Anorexia nervosa

The MFT approach to the treatment of anorexia nervosa owes a huge debt to Salvador Minuchin and his team in Philadelphia (Minuchin *et al.* 1978). These systemic pioneers, working with only one family at the time, created family interventions that are still, at least in part, influencing current practices. Their structural approach aimed to change family interactions and, above all, those taking place around eating and could be directly observed. The parents were centrally involved in helping their teenage children to put on weight and to encourage them to develop a healthier relationship to food. 'Lunchtime' sessions seemed the perfect scenario to observe family interactions in vivo and typical relationship problems were literally 'enacted' (Minuchin 1974) when the parents attempted to feed their adolescent children. Here disagreements between the parents, hidden alliances and open coalitions formed between the anorexic and one of the parents against the other, conflict avoidance on the parents' part, ill-defined boundaries between the generations all would become visible and they could then be challenged, 'perturbed' and changed by specific interventions (Minuchin and Fishman 1981). The therapeutic approach used by the Philadelphia team deliberately tried to 'unbalance' in favour of the parents, who were supported by the therapists to help their children to restore normal eating.

This work, inspirational though it was, has been modified over the years. Current MFT approaches (Schmidt and Asen 2005) as pioneered by the teams in Dresden (Scholz *et al.* 2005) and in London (Eisler *et al.* 2003; Eisler 2005) reflect these influences, as well as those of the Milan team (Selvini Palazzoli *et al.* 1980) and their circular questioning and the externalizing techniques (White and Epston 1990). A major aim is to increase parental efficacy by helping parents to adopt a primary role in taking charge of their child's illness, both during MFT and subsequently in the home setting. MFT for anorexia nervosa was started at the Child and Adolescent Psychiatry Department of the University of Dresden in November 1998 (Scholz and Asen 2001). Soon after, in spring 1999, a similar project took off at the Maudsley Hospital in London (Dare and Eisler 2000). Both teams have over the years experimented with a range of different lengths and frequencies of MFT programmes. In Dresden up to eight families are treated together by two therapists, with 20 whole days spread out over a whole year (see Table 8.2, p. 126). The work starts with an intensive four days, all during the course of one week, followed by further whole days in increasing intervals. In between the multi-family treatment days, single family work can be offered if required, but is rarely necessary. The Maudsley team uses a less intense MFT programme, lasting for a period of nine months, with only 10–12 whole days. The work also starts with a 'burst' of four whole days and an initial follow-up after 1–2 weeks, followed by whole day MFT once every 4–6 weeks. During MFT the main aims for the parents are as follows:

- to overcome the illness-related isolation of the family
- to take on responsibility for managing the illness-specific symptoms and everyday situations
- to connect with other parents to share experiences and strategies
- to improve intra-familial conflict management
- to strengthen parental bonds with children and develop conciliation skills
- to change problematic interactions and relationship patterns around their child's eating
- to address personal psychological issues if these affect the child's specific problems adversely.

The aims of the anorectic teenagers are:

- to improve their ability to be emotionally closer to their parents whilst permitting them to take responsibility for the anorectic's recovery
- to accept parental consequences and persistence as expressions of love and care, instead of demonizing or idealizing their parents
- to accept that they suffer from a serious illness, generate insight into the illness and decrease anorexic symptomatology
- to learn to accept responsibility for their own body and autonomy.

There are four distinct phases for MFT work with anorectics and their families. It starts with an *introductory afternoon/evening* (see Table 8.2, p. 126) which allows families to get a first 'taste' of MFT and to meet fellow sufferers and their families. It is helpful if families who have benefited from attending MFT groups in the past, or who are in the middle of one of those groups, present their experiences of participating in MFT. These 'graduate' or 'veteran' families give hope and prove to be invaluable for engaging reluctant or sceptical parents. It is best to hold the introductory event as late as possible in the afternoon, so as to make it possible for working parents to attend. Snacks and drinks are provided and placed prominently on a table to greet families as they arrive. Staff then welcome everyone formally, in the way described in Chapter 2. We are aware that there are teams which like to commence with a psycho-educational talk about anorexia nervosa, its aetiology, risks and treatment and dietary regimes, spiced with statistical data and research results. Instead, we attempt to elicit ideas about these and other subjects directly from the families and their individual members. There is ample information already available in families who have plenty of experience with anorexia nervosa when the different ideas are pooled. After all, most families have struggled with anorexia nervosa for years. When 'veteran' families tell their stories this is usually a source of hope and encouragement for the 'new' families, providing a kind of preview of 'forthcoming attractions'! A question and answer slot follows, and we tend to involve families in responding to the questions rather than providing the answers ourselves. It is very rare that we are required to draw on our specialist knowledge, given that in a room with anorexia nervosa sufferers and their families there is much condensed experience. It is always very impressive how much these families know, and when it comes to discussing diets, calories, food additives and weight issues, there is very little that a professionally trained dietician could add. After this slot there is a pause of 15 to 30 minutes, an informal time when families and their individual members can congregate around the table, staring at the snacks or indeed devouring them. This allows everyone to see how different families manage food. At some point during the introductory evening it is possible to show a short film entitled *Games Anorexia Plays*. We have a few different versions of this film, made over the years by different anorexia nervosa ex-sufferers and their parents. The film lasts approximately 15 minutes and shows vividly – and with some humour – how anorexia 'forces' teenagers to deceive their parents and professionals about their weight and eating. The group can be told that they can also consider making such a film at the end of their treatment. Over the years there have been new titles added to the repertoire, such as *How We Defeated Anorexia* or *Team Family vs Anorexia United*. These films stimulate discussion and, above all, provide hope that the illness can be overcome. This approach is clearly inspired by externalization concepts and techniques as put forward by White and Epston (1990): anorexia is defined as an enemy that has to be defeated.

The second stage of MFT – which lasts about three months – could be called the *symptom-oriented phase* (see Table 8.2, p. 126). Here the focus is rather narrow and concerns itself above all with increasing weight, the preparation of food and eating. One major aim is to increase the parents' motivation and skills and to get them to take charge of the anorexia. As all parents have very similar struggles with their offspring, the group of parents quickly knits together. They compare notes, they share experiences and support each other. The anorectic teenager can experience this as quite overwhelming – instead of merely battling her own parents, she now also has to put up with the pressure other parents exert. The parents are continually encouraged to take full responsibility for their children's eating and their interactions around food, by setting appropriate boundaries and by not getting involved in endless negotiations with regard to how much needs to be eaten within what time. At the same time, they need to be supported in gaining more confidence and not letting the illness defeat them. It is hard for parents to be present during all the meals without the possibility of offloading their responsibility to staff. Many problems to do with intra-family communication and inter-actions manifest themselves around the eating issues, and this remains the primary focus during the first three months of the work. Any other family or individual problems, in the index patient or other family members, are delib-erately not privileged during this phase. It is the therapist's task to refocus the work and support the parents in their efforts to get their child to eat, and not to be drawn into role modelling or taking over altogether.

Food is loaded with multiple meanings in most families. It can be perceived as an expression of love, an act of care and nurture, but also sometimes as a substitute for love. These entail powerful emotions and the provision of food can be experienced by an anorectic teenager as the parent making a very special effort and at the same time punishing and possibly even 'torturing' the young person. Irrational though this may be, such a stance very much affects the parents and evokes strong and conflicting feelings, from feeling rejected, guilty and anxious, to being a failure and useless. These contradictory feel-ings can lead to paralysis. When parents meet the parents from other eating disordered adolescents in MFT groups, comparisons are invited, particularly when it comes to observing others during feeding times. If all six to eight families are seated around one huge table it is impossible not to become curious as to how the eating is handled elsewhere. Sooner rather than later parents and children comment and give each other feedback across the table. Such feedback is easier to take from fellow sufferers than from staff, and staff can soon afford to take a 'back seat' and observe the meals from a distance. We do not encourage staff to eat with the families as satisfying their own (biological) needs may distract them from their task of observing and inter-vening. Staff, in order to avoid becoming hypoglycaemic, will take turns in leaving the room and eat at their own pace and in peace elsewhere, with one therapist remaining in the room, ready to intervene if necessary.

The seeming inversion of hierarchies in families containing an anorectic teenager is most striking during mealtimes. They seem to be in charge of the family, with everyone dancing – or pussyfooting – around them. One can observe how compromises are being made by the parents and how they cave in when negotiating the quantities of food their offspring should eat. One can also listen to the consequences that the parents threaten and their utter inability to implement them. Spending more time with their child has two seemingly contradictory effects: there is more conflict and less 'pseudo-harmony' on the one hand, but also more closeness and emotional connectedness on the other. The therapists will focus on whether and how boundaries are set and how appropriate they are. They will draw attention to the continuous negotiations and renegotiations with regard to how much needs to be eaten – and when and where. It is here that peer support and pressure are most effective in promoting change all round. It can get very heated during eating times and is the most intensive part of the MFT work. Tears and laughter succeed each other from one minute to the next.

To achieve maximum intensity and change, each day during the symptom-related phase is very structured and requires families and their individual members continually to change context and to adapt to new demands, many of which have to do with food and eating (Table 8.1). This is both exhausting and frees energy, with families literally 'buzzing'. The initial eight to ten treatment days are very structured. There are not only specific multi-family group modules, with all families present in the same room at the same time, but also other groups which run in parallel – parents' groups, teenagers' groups, relaxation classes, shopping expeditions, food preparation, and so on. Once families become more self-assured, they are involved in co-designing the programme for each day and at a later stage they may well be in charge of each day.

During the *relationship-oriented phase* of MFT (see Table 8.2), the emphasis remains on the continuation of establishing healthier eating patterns and, most importantly, to achieve adequate weight gain and maintenance. Hence each day continues to start with the weighing of the anorectic and this frequently sets the mood for the day. Some adolescents simply do not want their parents to know their actual weight, others do not want to know it themselves. Staff insist on the weighing, above all to ensure that the anorectic is not in a life-threatening condition. Discussing the weight – or discussing the reasons for why the weight should be kept secret – is important, and

Table 8.1 Timetable for typical MFT day

8.45 Weighing
9.00 Breakfast
9.30 Multi-family exercise
11.00 Reflective group
12.00 Lunch preparation, eating and clearing up
13.15 Informal time
13.45 Video feedback session
15.00 Speed dating
16.00 Tea and biscuits
16.30 Finish

Table 8.2 Treatment plan for anorexia nervosa MFT

Time plan	Therapeutic focus	Exercises
Phase 1: Introductory evening		
2–3 hours	* Learning about MFT * Exchanging experiences * Planning programme	• Connecting families • Speed dating • Tricks and knacks • Psycho-self-education
Phase 2: Symptom-oriented		

1 week later
5 days
3 weeks later
3 days
	* Increasing parental
	  responsibility
	* Increasing motivation
	* Identifying and implementing
	  parental consequences
	* Boundary setting
	* Focusing on problematic
	  interactions around eating
	  and weighing
	* Increasing weight
		• Joint meals
		• Food collage
		• Adoptive meal
		• Third breakfast
		• Body image poster
		• Letters to illness
		• Goal trees

Phase 3: Relationship-oriented		

4 weeks later
2 days
4 weeks later
2 days
After another 4 weeks
1 day per month
	* Family relationships
	* Examining expressed emotion
	* Challenging unhelpful
	  hierarchies
	* Addressing communication
	  issues
	* Challenging enmeshment
		• Live sculpting
		• Life river
		• Mind scanning
		• Family trees
		• Anonymous letters
		• Posters and films
		• Press conference
		• Memory lane
		• Life after serious accident
		• Friction generates warmth

Phase 4: Future-oriented		
Months 10–12 **3 × 1 day**	* Managing stagnation * Preventing relapse * Addressing autonomy issues	• Outing (restaurant) • Masks • Hypothetical scenarios • Finishing

different families and their individual members have very diverse ideas about this important topic. However, the themes addressed during this phase of MFT gradually shift to more general intra-family relationships. These include issues to do with family hierarchy, possible triangulation of the anorectic teenager, specific communication disturbances, inappropriate emotional involvement, covert coalitions and real or imagined secrets. In this phase the 'place' and 'role' of anorexia in the immediate and wider family context are explored and addressed. Available internal and external resources are identified and the family is encouraged to consider how to make good use of these. New specific goals are also identified. Long-term and transgenerational family patterns are examined. Systemic work during this phase is increasingly less illness specific and deals with family relationship issues as they present themselves. However, there is still also an emphasis on eating and on maintaining a healthy weight.

The fourth phase is *future-oriented* (see Table 8.2) and concerns itself with how to maintain the progress achieved and how to identify warning signs that there may be an impending relapse. This is often linked to issues of the personal autonomy of the anorectic, including who is responsible for her body and health. The consequences of increased independence are explored and plans for the future are made. During this phase there are many discussions with regard to what constitutes a 'minimum healthy weight' and the fact that sustaining this is not equivalent to a 'cure'.

The Dresden MFT model is not all that different from the approach developed by the team at the Maudsley Hospital in London (Eisler *et al.* 2003). However, one major difference is that the London team works in less confrontational ways during the symptom-specific phase. There is less emphasis on having joint meals or making elaborate eating plans and more of a focus on discussion groups and reflections. Work has also been undertaken in the adult field with chronic anorexia nervosa sufferers (Colahan and Robinson 2002). Over the past ten years MFT for adolescent anorexia nervosa has become increasingly popular, with teams in Canada, China, Denmark, France, Netherlands, Norway, Sweden and Switzerland, working in this way both in inpatient and day hospital settings. There are various outpatient projects which are of interest. In Paris, for example, a team (Cook-Darzens and Doyen 2006) offers a half-open group for five to seven families which meets once a fortnight for two hours over a period of nine months. This amounts to an average of 18 sessions and a sequence consisting of a block of two sessions of parallel work with parents and children, followed by a joint session with whole families being present. Similar work also takes place in England, mostly in outpatient settings of existing child and adolescent mental health services, usually with the less severely affected anorexia nervosa sufferers (Dalley 2008). However, in contrast to the Parisian project, it is always whole families that attend for each session. These last two hours each, and whilst it is for pragmatic reasons usually not possible to prepare and eat lunch, the provision of snacks and drinks that are brought in halfway through sessions proves to be an important focus around which eating issues are discussed concretely. There is the possibility of undertaking parallel work with adults and children in separate groups, followed by reflective work in the large group.

Bulimia nervosa

The MFT approach with normal-weight bulimic adolescents is quite different from the work with anorexia nervosa sufferers and their families. This is due to the fact that by the time bulimic teenagers seek and receive treatment, the illness has been present for years. On average, normal weight bulimics are considerably older than their anorectic 'colleagues' and involving their parents proves more problematic. Furthermore, binge eating and purging is usually a much more secret affair and thus can be concealed better and for longer. Bulimics also tend to have strong feelings of shame and embarrassment and this further compounds the delayed identification. As compared with anorexia nervosa, which tends to (also) be glorified by its sufferers, bulimia sufferers are often literally nauseated by their illness and show considerable self-hatred – much more overtly than anorexia nervosa sufferers. The motivation to change bulimic behaviours is much less marked in these families, above all because the illness is less obviously life threatening. As it is a much more secret illness than anorexia nervosa, the parents of bulimia nervosa sufferers are much more in the dark about the serious medical long-term effects.

The first phase of MFT is symptom and illness oriented and focuses on negotiating parental control over eating and weight-related behaviours, and a major purpose is to establish a therapeutic alliance with all members of the family (Le Grange and Lock 2007). It is only once progress has been made that the control over eating and weight is gradually handed back to the adolescent, but under the supervision of the parents. In this second phase, relationship issues and individual problems that 'feed bulimia' are explored, as well as the likely negative long-term effects. In the symptom-oriented phase MFT work concentrates on changing bulimic behaviours via:

- introducing regular and frequent, sufficiently nutritious meals, with small portions
- identifying triggers and contexts for binge and purge episodes
- devising strategies to reduce/avoid these
- putting in place parental supervision at critical times, above all before and after mealtimes, as well as at other defined crisis points
- changing food storage, display and availability of food in the family home
- insisting on family meals when all members eat together.

The aims for the parents are:

- to overcome family isolation
- to improve intra-familal conflict resolution
- to increase intra-familial bonds between parents and adolescents

- to improve 'making up' – reconciliation
- to change problematic interactions around eating
- to address their own difficulties managing the symptoms of their children and their own emotional states arising from these.

The aims for the bulimic patients are:

- to become responsible for implementing techniques that address symptom reduction
- to accept parental support
- to accept responsibility for their own health and body.

MFT with normal weight bulimics has proved much more difficult than the work with anorexia nervosa sufferers and their families. We have found that it is unrealistic to expect that the parents will commit themselves to attend each time and, as a result, we are now offering fortnightly groups for only the bulimic teenagers, for two hours on each occasion. Once every six weeks there is a whole day when parents and other family members join the group for a whole multi-family day. The work spans one year. As the parents are often literally 'in the dark' about the illness, psycho-education plays a more important role here than in MFT work with other conditions and problems, an observation also made by other teams (Wooley and Lewis 1987). MFT with this client group can only be regarded as an add-on to other more evidenced-based treatments.

Childhood obesity

Childhood obesity is a growing concern in many countries and over the past few years MFT projects for obese children and their families have been developed in the Netherlands, Germany and England. As childhood obesity is linked with lifestyle factors such as poor diet and lack of exercise, MFT has to involve parents and other significant carers in central ways. MFT projects for this client group all have a joint focus on eating, exercise and other healthy living practices, as well as exploring emotional issues connected with obesity. The very title of the 'Gut Feelings' project at the Marlborough Family Service in London reflects the link between emotional problems and overeating. These children are not only hugely overweight, but they also do present with emotional and behavioural problems in various different contexts. Typically they are bullied in school and their eating patterns cause a lot of conflict in the family home. Almost all the children have poor self-esteem and low mood. Many of the children are not at all motivated to lose weight, as 'comfort eating' is their way of silencing unwanted feelings. This is often in the context of a long history of general practitioners and paediatricians, school nurses and dieticians having pointed out the huge health risks to the child. We have found that it is less difficult to work with pre-adolescent children, as obesity and the interactions around it are less chronic and less entrenched.

The Gut Feelings MFT programme consists of fortnightly sessions, each lasting two and a half hours from 9.00–11.30. Families are encouraged to attend for one year. The first 45 minutes are used for the formal discussion of a specific topic, initially nominated by staff and subsequently by the families. Topics include: bullying because of being fat ('fat' is the term which the children use to describe themselves); lack of confidence; society's and personal ideas about obesity; being judged by one's physical appearance and how to counteract this; portion sizes; behaviour management around food; 'to nag or not to nag'; the pros and cons of food diaries; different beliefs about food among family members; linking eating to emotions; parental guilt; food denial.

The following 45 minutes are taken up by activities which involve and engage both parents and children. These have to be fun and energetic at the same time, without being seen as exercise or too physically demanding. It is crucial that parents and children take part in something 'physical' together. The games played include: egg and spoon races; three-legged races; negotiating an obstacle course (designed by one of the children) which is timed; football, volleyball, musical chairs, musical statues, and so on. An adapted version of 'Snakes and Ladders' has also proved popular, with the 'snake' having to eat vegetables chosen by the parent and the 'ladder' representing the eating of a new fruit. The winners can negotiate a joint activity with their respective families.

This is followed by a 15-minute break during which there is plenty of temptation for the parents to provide 'snacks' for the children who are often very demanding, pointing out the loss of energy incurred by the physical activity. Here then is an opportunity to deal 'live' with issues of 'stuffing yourself' – and being 'stuffed' and 'shut up'. The remaining 45 minutes of the session can be used for role plays or other activities and exercises. Role plays are chosen by parent and child together. Examples are how to manage difficult behaviour around food, with parents and children first playing themselves and then swapping roles; how to deal with being bullied, with children taking turns at being the bully or doing the bullying. Homework tasks can also be identified during this time slot, such as food diaries, portion sizes, breakfast charts, or change of diet. Outcome measures used include children's and parents' weight and height measured at the start and then at four-monthly intervals; SDQ and well-being questionnaires at the beginning and end of MFT; and client satisfaction questionnaires.

Schizophrenia and other psychotic disorders

MFT for people with schizophrenia and their families has been around for more than half a century. We have already described in the first chapter how this approach was initially developed by Laqueur and his colleagues (Laqueur *et al.* 1964) and subsequently by the team around W. R. McFarlane (McFarlane 1993; McFarlane 2002). A major aspect of the work is to increase the families' coping skills in managing symptoms, vulnerability and disability. Much of this work is psycho-educational in essence and aims to actively reduce the key relatives' levels of expressed emotion (EE), above all the critical comments and overinvolvement (Leff and Vaughn 1985). The approach is based on the assumption that families can 'learn' or be 'taught' what they do not 'know'. The major ideas underpinning the psycho-educational model is that over time families can develop methods of dealing with positive and negative symptoms, mostly via painful trial and error. It is also postulated that they find ways of dealing with positive and negative symptoms, as well as learning to manage functional disabilities and carer burden. However, psycho-educationalists argue that the resulting coping skills are dysfunctional and 'counterintuitive' and therefore more functional ones need to be taught (McFarlane 2002). The psycho-educational approach holds that families containing a person with psychosis need to possess all the available knowledge about the illness and the treatment team is seen as being the major source of that information, teaching 'lessons' which will help to affect and change predominantly the carers' behaviours. Another major emphasis in McFarlane's approach is on problem solving, addressing commonly encountered problems such as: family conflicts; aggressive and suicidal behaviours; compliance with medication; substance and alcohol misuse; as well as complying with medical advice and prescribed medication regimes. In each MFT session a specific problem is selected and all group members are invited to list all possible solutions. They are then encouraged to discuss the advantages and disadvantages of each solution in turn and finally choose the solution that best fits the situation, with a detailed plan as to how to implement it (McFarlane 2002).

Impressive though McFarlane's work and research is, his team's strong emphasis on formal psycho-education and problem-solving approaches does not quite 'fit' with our model of systemic practices and our long and extensive experience with practising MFT, as developed in London and Dresden. One of the main points of our approach is to activate the families' own resources and to elicit their own, often buried, knowledge and 'know-how'. With the help of the internet, books, magazines and other publications, families are now in a much better position to have access to relevant information than was the case only a few decades ago. In addition, families can also inspire each other, and some of the best (unscripted) psycho-education is 'family to family'. It has to be stressed that our MFT approach for working with psychotic adolescents and adults has been developed via outpatient work and in collaboration with colleagues from acute psychiatry, rather than being based in mental hospitals as an 'add-on' to institutional(ized) practices (Asen and Schuff 2006).

It must be obvious that when working with clients with severe and enduring mental health issues and their relevant services there is considerable potential for major clashes between a 'pure' medical model and the bio-psychosocial 'systemic' model, with its emphasis on seeing and treating people and ill health in context. Without finding ways of bridging the two worlds, there is little hope of systemic practitioners effecting change and a great risk that the psychotic person and his or her family will fall into the gap. This is why, from the outset, systemic practitioners need to accept the 'official' diagnosis, even if they perceive this as being painfully 'linear' or even a 'social construction'. They also need to accept the (already) prescribed treatment which usually relies heavily on antipsychotic medication. It is usually the case that psychotic clients and their families, particularly if they are long-term sufferers and labelled as 'chronic', will often 'live' the diagnosis and tend to feel lost if the illness is dismissed or is deconstructed overnight.

Prior to starting MFT, families with psychotic members require some preparation. This takes the form of meeting with each family on their own on three occasions, ideally in the presence of a professional from the local community mental health team (CMHT) who is already connected with the family. These single family meetings promote understanding of the particular issues with which the family is struggling and help family members to feel listened to and understood. It is our experience that engagement in sub-sequent MFT work is hugely increased via these initial encounters and non-attendance or early drop-out rates are significantly reduced. Once six to eight families have been recruited, one can start the actual MFT work with an initial whole-day 'workshop'. The term 'workshop' is chosen to emphasize that this is not a formal psycho-educational 'course', or 'therapy'. This day is very structured, with formal presentations on specific themes (such as diagnosis, stigma, medication, treatments and therapies), followed by small group discussions and then lunch and other programmed opportunities for what may be termed 'informal socializing'. The day can be concluded with a final plenary, with families listing the 'survival skills' they have (re)discovered or learned from scratch. Good quality refreshments and a fairly light and good-humoured atmosphere of informality prove to be important ingredients for successful engagement. The workshop is followed by two-hour MFT sessions at fortnightly or three-weekly intervals. These work best in the late afternoon, as this permits family members with a job to attend as well.

The membership for this kind of MFT work does not need to be restricted to one particular diagnostic category, as the differences between conditions such as schizophrenia, bipolar or schizo-affective illness are not all that marked when it comes to considering the common problems of having to cope with radical changes in functioning; with problems of relating to others inside and outside the family; of treatment compliance or of having to solve specific problems related to the impact of mental illness on all those near and dear. It can also be important to have a wide range of group members' ages, ethnicities and family constellations. The age mix can assist the formation of ad hoc subgroups which can undertake some separate work in parallel. This could, for example, be a discussion group composed of young adults and a parallel group of older caring adults. The presence of families with a whole variety of ethnic origins and cultural roots can provide a unique opportunity to explore the meanings of symptoms and behaviours in different cultural settings. We have found that flexibility is important. Group members should be able to come and go as they wish and, as long as confidentiality rules are adhered to, they should also be able to bring new family members or friends to the group. This can also apply to the helping system: families can invite, for example, their community psychiatric nurse or their social worker. We think it is important that it is up to the families and their individual members to determine content, direction and duration of exchanges in the group, but often guidance by the therapists is important.

In MFT sessions much time is spent on whole-group discussions, sharing positive and negative experiences, identifying problems more clearly, and focusing on problem solving. A wide range of topics and issues is covered, above all in relation to understanding and negotiating emotional issues arising in communication and interaction, medication, double diagnosis, leaving home, carer burden, parental overinvolvement, couple issues, relapse prevention and crisis management. Staff can initiate playful MFT exercises, such as Mind Scanning (F8), Ten Family Commandments (F2), Clay Family Sculptures (F20), or Mood Barometer (F22). Families are also invited to bring special (food) dishes from their places or countries of origin, to talk about their specific customs and traditions, social and cultural expectations, as well as about their views on mental health problems and their meanings in different cultural settings.

Groups can be closed or semi-open, as an 'add-on' to ongoing psychopharmacological and cognitive behavioural interventions. MFT lends itself particularly to working with families in the early course of a psychotic disorder, when family members tend to be centrally involved and are still more open to participation. However, acutely psychotic patients are difficult to contain in MFT and if they relapse they will not attend MFT until their mental states are more settled. When attempting to adapt this model to the work with very chronic, institutionalized inpatients with schizophrenia in Italy, our colleagues in Milan found that it was more difficult to activate relatives who had many years ago handed over the care of their ill family members to mental hospital staff. With this client group family members have often become replaced by significant others, such as hostel staff or workers from voluntary organizations, and we have worked with them successfully in MFT.

We have already stressed that it is very important for MFT work to be embedded in the wider service context, even though the model supports the notion that the family is – or becomes – the main care provider. Local CMHTs are very frequently involved, and as MFT fosters collaborative and transparent interactions and communications among professionals, patients and carers, MFT group members are encouraged to use their respective psychiatric services as well, to have more of a say with regard to service provision and the shaping of 'their' treatments.

MFT is not always a smooth process and plenty of dynamics emerge which can be challenging for the therapists. For example, if one group member – a relative or patient – dominates the meeting, it is usually much easier for a member of staff to create appropriate boundaries than it is for other members of the group. On other occasions, a person with psychosis might become overwhelmed or confused by the group process: the therapist will then need to create appropriate mini-contexts to lower the quantity of stimuli and emotion. This can lead to setting up a brief small subgroup which allows space for the affected person. Staff may also, on very rare occasions, need to protect patients from being exposed to high EE comments and interactions from one of their relatives or from members of other families. However, this is, in our experience, a very rare event, as multi-family groups develop their own rules of 'good conduct'.

The 'Mental Health Matters Workshops' developed by Cooklin (2004) and his colleagues (Bishop *et al.* 2002) are another application of MFT, though the focus here is on the dependent children of parents who suffer from a major psychotic disorder. Initially they were presented as 'one-off' events but repeated on average every six weeks, lasting six hours. Now the workshop is an 'open group', with up to ten or fifteen families being 'on the roll' and with the majority of people attending regularly and over a considerable length of time. Each workshop has a theme, such as 'diagnosis', 'treatment', 'voices groups' or 'young carers'. It is conducted in quite a structured way, starting with a formal presentation, followed by small group discussions, a reflecting plenary, mid-work workshop evaluation, joint lunch, further group discussions and other activities. This approach has in recent years been modified and focuses on the children of chronically mentally ill parents. Workshops now take place once a month in the late afternoon, for two hours. The aim is to help parents to understand the positions and dilemmas of their children and for the children to understand what mental illness is. In this workshop children and parents are initially separated. The parents have a discussion group around a theme and the children, with the help of a therapist, write mini theatre plays and sketches which have specific themes, such as 'living with the illness', 'when help is not helpful', 'when nobody listens', 'fear', etc. This preparatory work takes about one hour, including rehearsal time. The sketches are then performed in front of the parents or, if a little film has been made, this is shown to them. This is followed by a discussion exploring the themes and connecting these to the parents' group which had gone on in parallel to the children's group. Sometimes families make overt links with issues portrayed in the play and the reality at home, at other times it is just left for people to draw their own conclusions.

Depression and mood disorders

Over the years we have noticed that a significant number of parents participating in MFT programmes suffered from depression, some diagnosed 'officially' and others not. However, in those cases depression was generally not the main presenting problem and generally not the reason for being referred to MFT. Instead, the referral had been triggered by a child's emotional or behavioural difficulties, by an adult with a major psychotic disorder, or by a family that has been labelled as 'highly dysfunctional'. Over the years we discovered that even if the depression of a parent was not overtly treated, most parents' mental states benefited from participating in MFT. Being in the company of other parents and developing close and confiding relationships with a parent of the same gender is known to be a protective factor against depression (Brown and Harris 1978), and the formation of friendship networks as the result of MFT work is a well-documented outcome of this type of work. Many parents have told us that after participating in an MFT group they stopped taking their antidepressant medication and felt generally better about themselves, having gained new self-confidence and also valuing themselves more. In other words, MFT often has good 'side effects' on parents' mental states – even if these are not the primary target.

MFT for mood disorders has been in place for some years, including for bipolar disorder (Keitner *et al.* 2002). Much of this work has a strong psychoeducational focus, including group work with relatives (Harter *et al.* 2002; Keller and Schuler 2002). A more recent development in Belgium (Lemmens *et al.* 2007, 2009b) combines MFT with systemic couple therapy (Asen and Jones 1999; Jones and Asen 2000). The work consists of seven sessions, with most sessions being attended by the couples only and a few sessions when dependent children are also present. Sessions first focus on the impact of depression on the couple and on their children. Then attempts are made to restore family functioning via sessions with the couple, as well as in sessions when the children are present. A relapse prevention session then takes place, with one follow-up session three months later. Sessions last 90 minutes, the work takes place over two to three months and requires two therapists.

Chapter 9

Pragmatic considerations

In this chapter we discuss a range of questions that we frequently encounter. These concern a variety of issues, from research to work settings and institutional structures, from training issues to ground rules that need to be observed when undertaking MFT, from the use of interpreters to likely future developments in the field.

The effectiveness and efficacy of MFT

Increasingly, clinicians need to demonstrate 'what works for whom under what conditions' and this also applies to MFT if it wants to be a member of the 'evidenced-based club' (Larner 2004). This is not an easy task as it is difficult for most therapists working in public services to undertake randomized controlled trials (RCTs) which require manualization and controlled replication by independent researchers. Nevertheless, to date there are more than 40 RCTs examining the effectiveness and efficacy of MFT and comparing this approach to other treatments. In addition, there are plenty of other studies which, however, do not reach the 'gold standard' of RCTs. While it can be said that RCTs have a high internal validity, their transferability to ordinary clinical settings makes their external validity rather limited. In addition, RCTs are of considerable importance in knowing what works, but much less is known about how MFT works and how different factors interact to enhance or interfere with the process of change (Eisler 2006). This understanding would be increased by using other research designs – from single case studies to process research, dismantling studies and experimental designs. Naturalistic and single case studies often have a higher relevance for therapists, as they can throw light on the actual process of therapy, but from a scientific point of view they sadly have only stepchildren status. A positive development is the emergence of 'user-led research' which involves current clients and ex-clients as research partners and 'experts by experience'. They work together with clinicians to determine content and aims of research projects, aims that are relevant for them and not just merely for scientists inhabiting ivory towers. Service user involvement in research very much fits the ethos of MFT, drawing on the resources and experiences – and the different perspectives – of 'veteran' families.

Most research projects concerned with outcome tend to measure the presence, reduction or absence of disorder-specific symptoms, cost effectiveness of the intervention, reduction of carer burden and treatment acceptability, as well as the appropriateness of an intervention for clients from different cultural and ethnic backgrounds. In all these dimensions MFT can demonstrate good results, be that to do with treatment efficacy, effectiveness or efficiency. There are discussions as to whether some of the psycho-educational MFT projects and studies should be included in the evidence base or not, as it is at times argued that they are not sufficiently systemic. We have a less purist view and believe that, no matter what some of its theoretical tenets, in practice many aspects of this work look remarkably 'systemic'. What all MFT approaches have in common, be they behavioural or not, is that they involve families in their own recovery.

The 'politics of evidence' (Larner 2004) nevertheless require us to cite RCTs as the most acceptable research data – with funding implications. Most RCTs in the field of MFT focus on illnesses or disorders in the field of adult psychiatry. There are more than 20 studies examining the effects of MFT on people with schizophrenia and their families (for example, McFarlane *et al.* 1995a, 1995b; Dyck *et al.* 2000, 2002; Hazel *et al.* 2004; Bradley *et al.* 2006; McDonell *et al.* 2006). These demonstrate that the relapse rate of patients with schizophrenia can be reduced by 50 per cent if MFT is used in conjunction with medication, as compared with treatments that rely predominantly on psychotropic medication alone. With adjuvant MFT treatment persons with schizophrenia also show a significant improvement in social interactions and employment opportunities. In addition, family members are more able to manage the illness and there is a marked reduction of carer burden. Last but not least, it has been shown that the combined MFT and medication approach is less time consuming and cheaper than relying mainly on medication only. Interestingly – and perhaps depressingly – these well-supported scientific findings have still not resulted in a change of practice in the majority of adult psychiatry services: family intervention, be that in the form of MFT or single family therapy, tends to be a rare rather than a standard treatment for schizophrenia.

More than half a dozen studies show that MFT can also be successful in the treatment of *alcohol dependence* (McCrady *et al.* 1979; Bowers and Al-Redha 1990; Monti *et al.* 1990; O'Farrell *et al.* 1985, 1992, 1993, 1998; Fals-Stewart *et al.* 2005, 2006). This usually takes the form of multi-couple therapy and relies heavily on the use of behavioural techniques. Typical positive treatment outcomes are reduction of alcohol consumption and higher rates of subsequent abstinence, as compared with other treatment approaches.

Some studies also show that MFT can be helpful with *mood disorders*, with a reduction of expressed emotion (Leff and Vaughn 1985) and critical comments in particular, as well as a reduction in carer burden (Keitner *et al.* 2002; Harter *et al.* 2002; Keller and Schuler 2002). To date only two studies have examined symptom reduction, with one study showing a significant reduction of depressive symptomatology (Lemmens *et al.* 2007, 2009a) and another where this was not the case (Miller *et al.* 2004). There is also evidence that a combination of dialectical behaviour therapy and MFT is effective in reducing suicidal ideation in self-harming adolescents (Rathus and Miller 2002; Miller *et al.* 2007).

MFT for adolescent *anorexia nervosa* looks to be a very promising approach, though the results of a recent multicentre RCT (Eisler 2005) have not yet been published. Two completed trials (Geist *et al.* 2000; Rhodes *et al.* 2008) suggest that MFT (or a variation thereof, 'parent-to-parent consultation') relatively quickly reduces anorectic symptoms and carer burden; that intra-family relationships improve; that the treatment is very acceptable and that there are no negative side effects. Outcome and follow-up studies in Dresden (Thömke 2005; Döhler 2008) confirm these results and also show that mothers become more self-confident and self-assured and that their couple relationships become more stabilized – perhaps an important ingredient for the necessary parental competence required to manage the illness. MFT also appears to play a role in increasing the anorexia nervosa sufferers' independence and six months after the end of MFT patients have the same weight as those who had been treated as inpatients, but with weights remaining significantly more stable subsequently and a significantly reduced relapse rate (Thömke 2005; Döhler 2008).

In the last two decades, clinicians from the Marlborough Family Service have also examined effects and efficacy of MFT and found many positive effects, such as that MFT reduces symptoms, is highly acceptable and has low drop-out rates (e.g. Summer 1998; Singh 2000; Potter 2007). However, as most of these studies were retrospective, one needs to exercise considerable caution to interpret the results and make any general claims. It has to be pointed out that research in a busy public service is much more difficult to conduct than in university settings which are more geared to this type of enquiry. RCTs can often not be implemented by community-based services and clinics as local service level agreements and commitments do not allow that some clients and their families are excluded, via randomization, from receiving a specific service which is there for everybody living in the clinic's catchment area. For example, it has literally proved impossible to set up an RCT to evaluate the outcome of the Marlborough's Family School and Family Classroom projects as the service is contracted to provide this service for all local residents. It has been very difficult to devise a prospective study, examining the effects of school-based MFT, as the search for a matched control group in neighbouring London boroughs was met with reluctance, as there was huge reluctance for their outcomes to be compared, possibly unfavourably, with the Marlborough's MFT approach. Research in the public domain is often a bit of an obstacle race.

A different difficulty in undertaking 'pure' research and RCTs has arisen in Dresden. Here and in the rest of that part of eastern Germany, MFT for the treatment of adolescent anorexia nervosa has become well publicized over the past few years, mostly via a series of television programmes, newspaper and magazine articles. As a result, many families referred to the clinic wanted MFT, the 'real' thing as they perceived it, rather than being randomized and running the risk of being allocated to a control group. Research carried out in the Dresden Family Day Clinic has demonstrated that children between three and 13 years of age, presenting with emotional and behavioural disorders, showed significant symptomatic improvements after treatment which had only lasted between six and eight weeks. Their mothers were found to have increased self-confidence and to be able to apply consequences more consistently. The children did not experience this as withdrawal of love, but described their mothers as being more loving by the end of treatment. This would seem to confirm that children do not experience parental discipline and consistency as harshness or rejection, but as signs of genuine concern and love (Süß-Falkenberg 2005). Interestingly, the Dresden researchers also found that the parents of these children had less self-confidence in relation to their children and their parenting capacity than the parents of children presenting with depression or anorexia nervosa (Rix 2002). The team also found that about half of mothers attending the Dresden FDC had a diagnosable psychiatric disorder and that there had been no change by the end of attending MFT (which only lasted six to eight weeks). However, at 18 months follow-up the children's symptoms were found to be further reduced, a sign that the results of MFT are stable and an indication of the reduced relapse rate. As far as the mothers' symptoms were concerned, these did not improve significantly after the cessation of MFT but no differences between them and the control group were found at 18 months follow-up. This is a particularly encouraging result, given that no further treatments (medication or individual psychotherapy), other than single family therapy sessions, were offered after the end of MFT (Süß-Falkenberg 2005).

Which then are the important therapeutic processes and mechanisms of action underlying the positive effects of MFT? This is an area which has to date only been researched in a rather limited way. It has been argued (Asay and Lambert 1999; Miller and Duncan 2000) that the client's expectation and hope for change accounted for 15 per cent, the therapeutic relationship for 30 per cent and non-specific factors (client resourcefulness and chance events) for 40 per cent of the outcome of any psychotherapeutic approach. In other words, most of the variance for therapy outcome is covered by the common ground between all therapies. Various clinicians and researchers have described other factors for which there is some empirical support: experiencing communality; learning by observation; experiencing hope and support from the group; peer confrontation; experimenting with new ways of coping and relating; gaining multiple insights and expanding social networks. In a recent study Lemmens *et al.* (2009b) explored the specific therapeutic factors consistently associated with improvements in the presenting symptoms, in this case low mood. They found that, as far as the patients themselves were concerned, these were: making progress in trying out new behaviours; modelling (i.e. observing other people's responses) and getting guidance from the therapists. Other factors linked to outcome were: gaining insight into the partner's wishes; becoming aware that one can determine one's own life; self-disclosure; having confidence in the therapist; and learning by observing others working on their own problems. The partners of the depressed patients, on the other hand, identified the following helpful factors: feeling accepted (by the group) and gaining confidence in helping others; gaining insight about the connections between current behaviours and feelings and childhood experiences; and experiencing the support from the group (Lemmens *et al.* 2009b). This study also specifically enquired about unhelpful or disturbing events during MFT and found that multi-family therapy is generally well accepted, with few or no disturbing experiences (as also found by Anderson *et al.* 1986; Scholz *et al.* 2005) and high levels of treatment satisfaction (Lemmens *et al.* 2009b). The emergence of 'service user-led research' (Faulkner and Thomas 2002), with clients participating centrally in the design and evaluation of research projects, is a promising development, in line with the overall philosophy of MFT.

Clearly there is a great need to undertake more research to know '*what to do with whom when*'. Questions which can help researchers to inform future research on MFT are as follows:

1   What are the clinical aims of MFT in a specific group of families (at an individual, family and wider systems level)?
2   Which of the aims are most important (i.e. primary outcomes) and which are less important (i.e. secondary outcomes)?
3   What are the important changes that happen during MFT which help to achieve the aims (i.e. the potential mediators of treatment)?
4   Which individuals/families benefit most from MFT (i.e. predictors or moderators of treatment)? This can be assessed at an individual level (e.g. symptoms, co-morbidity, coping, quality of life), at a family level (e.g. improved relationships, conflicts, change in EE) or at a larger systems level (e.g. cost to society, employment).

Staffing issues and work settings

How many MFT therapists are needed to work with six to eight families? This question does not have one simple, straightforward answer as it very much depends on the work context and the specific issues and problems which MFT is meant to address. On average it is possible to undertake MFT with only two therapists – one who is the active therapist and the other who is essentially in an observer position. However, these two roles can be switched over and in experienced teams this may happen seamlessly in the middle of a group session. The observing therapist can be in the treatment room, behind a one-way screen or viewing the work on a television monitor, observing 'live'. In intensive MFT day settings, namely when families attend for whole days, one tends to employ more staff. For example, the FDU in London now employs five systemically trained family workers, as the often very complex work with multiproblem families requires more detailed observation and intervention, particularly when part of the task is to write elaborate expert reports for the courts. Here each family worker is the key worker for up to three families at any point in time. While there are five full-time therapists working in the FDU, we have found that there is less 'burn-out' if these therapists also undertake other clinical work – and on average 25 per cent of their time is spent working with single families in another part of the clinic. In addition to the full-time family workers, the FDU also receives supervisory input from members of the Marlborough's multidisciplinary team: psychiatry (two sessions or one day per week), psychology (two sessions) and child psychotherapy (two sessions).

Other day settings may have an even higher staff contingent, like the FDC in Dresden: here there is one full-time member of staff per family. Professionals are recruited mostly from nursing; there is full-time input from a psychiatrist and psychologist each, as well as art/occupational therapy (two days per week) and additional 'alternative' therapy time, in the form of therapeutic horse riding (half a day per week). Teachers are employed for ten hours per week. By contrast, the MFT programme for anorexia nervosa in Dresden only employs two family therapists who are not only responsible for the actual MFT work, with between four to seven groups per year, but also for the initial assessments, single family work and post-MFT work. There is some psychiatric input (two sessions per week). Other MFT programmes for eating disordered clients employ up to four family therapists and have a larger sessional input by psychiatrists and psychologists.

As a general rule we have found that most MFT work can be carried out by two therapists. However, depending on the complexity of the work – including carrying out difficult assessments for the courts, or dealing with complex multiproblem families – we recommend at least three full-time systemically trained staff, also to allow for sickness leave or holidays. Having too many staff present during MFT sessions can have a paralyzing effect on families. It is also difficult for each staff member to know what to do and to have a useful role, there being a temptation to do something merely to justify one's presence.

Apart from staff, MFT also requires the use of a room which is big enough to accommodate six to eight families. One room may only be sufficient for carrying out MFT projects which take place for two to three hours on a fortnightly or monthly basis. MFT work in day settings requires more than just one room. The FDC in Dresden, for example, can cater for up to six families which, including staff, can mean a 'crowd' of 25 people. The clinic has two group rooms that are both big enough to accommodate up to 30 people. One of these rooms is used as a general room for meetings and activities, the other has a huge table around which families can sit and do a range of exercises which involve drawing, painting, sticking or writing. The FDU in London also has two large rooms, one of which is equipped as a playroom, with many toys, games and climbing frames. The other room has a variety of uses, including MFT activities and exercises, but also for the families to eat in. Both the London and Dresden day units have a kitchen and in London the families themselves have to provide their own ingredients and prepare all the meals. Apart from several toilets, including some adapted specifically for children, each clinic has a staffroom, as well as a room in which parents or children participate in group work or where single family work can take place. In London there is also a room for infants, equipped with a number of cots and baby alarms. In Dresden there is a small 'ball bath' room, an area in which children can not only let off steam but also play about with their parents and experience physical contact with them. As both units are located in the basement of their respective institutions, there is easy access to a garden which can also be used for play and exercises. Cameras are mounted in most rooms, including the kitchen, so that video or DVD recordings can be made and later be viewed during audiovisual feedback sessions. We have seen similar spatial settings and arrangements in other units in Scandinavia, Belgium, France and other countries.

To work in day settings with eating disordered teenagers and their families, one needs two large rooms, a kitchen, as well as toilets. Units that we have seen in different countries and counties have quite different structures and conditions – and many have to double up for other work when they are not in use. As families containing eating disordered children and teenagers do not spend weeks and months in a day setting, it is less important to have a purpose-built structure and setting for this type of work. By contrast, the Family School based at the Marlborough Family Service is clearly an educational setting, equipped with modern learning and teaching tools, and has become a prototype for similar projects in other parts of Europe. It is located in a purpose-built construction in the grounds of the clinic and consists of one large room which is divided into two parts. One part very much resembles a classroom, with school desks and chairs, with other chairs placed away from the learning 'zone', used by the parents to allow them to observe the classroom interactions. The other part of the room is used for MFT group meetings and can easily accommodate 30 persons. Apart from two small staffrooms, there is another room which can be used for individual, couple or single family work. The unit also has toilets and limited kitchen facilities and there is access to the clinic garden during break times. This has a play area as well as two swings which pupils have to share. This requires them to take turns and negotiate who can use what equipment at what time. The parents are in attendance during break time, talking to each other and taking their child to task if they display disrespectful or unruly behaviours.

In summary, one of the important principles for carrying out MFT is to make the physical context resemble a naturalistic setting as much as possible. The day settings evoke some kind of 'home' atmosphere and the Family School does to some extent resemble a classroom. Whilst good physical and spatial conditions are important for MFT, many services do not have big rooms, let alone a dedicated MFT unit. Nevertheless, we know of many MFT projects that are carried out in improvised settings or rely on the goodwill of other services which do have access to large rooms. For example, rooms in schools may be used after school hours, community centres tend to have large rooms, as do some social services settings. Churches and other religious institutions often offer their premises for MFT.

Institutional and wider system structures

In this book we have provided ample examples of how it is possible to manage highly symptomatic and very problematic individuals – children, adolescents and adults – in multi-family day units or clinics. Compared with inpatient treatments, day-setting based MFT needs fewer staff as there is no need for a shift system covering nights or weekends. As a result this form of treatment is less expensive for the severe end of disturbed individuals and their families and should therefore be more attractive to managers – even though health, education or social care employers in different places find this difficult to take on board. For example, in Dresden it has been demonstrated that pre-adolescent children with severe emotional and behavioural disorders can be helped without the need for inpatient admission, so much so that all inpatient beds for pre-adolescent children were closed a short while after the FDC started its work. However, the German system – health insurance based and plagued by bureaucratic rules and procedures – had huge problems finding ways of remunerating the clinic for what turned out to be much cheaper and at least equally effective assessment and therapeutic work. Paradoxically, the insurance companies – hardly charitable organizations – preferred to pay effectively three times as much for a child's inpatient treatment than they would for MFT. It was only when the University of Dresden sued one major German insurance company and won the litigation that MFT became an accepted and funded treatment – but only in Saxony and not (yet) in most other parts of Germany. This 'victory' made it possible also to charge for the work with the parents – who do not have to become 'patients' in their own right, but are now treated as 'medical escorts'. Furthermore, for those families who have to travel from far away, agreement has been reached that the insurance companies pay for all the family members' travel expenses, as well as hotel costs if they participated in daily MFT. The Dresden team has been able to demonstrate to health care politicians and administrators that, taking into account not only the actual MFT treatment costs but also the costs incurred if a child had to be admitted for inpatient treatment or be placed in foster care or a children's home, MFT provides a saving of between 40 and 60 per cent, depending on the severity of the case.

We have already mentioned that many parents who attend MFT with their children do themselves present with mental health issues. As they are 'treated' alongside their offspring, one could claim that such 'free' treatment would further reduce the overall costs of the 'family'. However, most health insurance companies all over the world would require considerable training to view financial issues from a systemic perspective. In countries with health services that are not (yet) based entirely on a health insurance system, like Great Britain and Scandinavian countries, it is – at least from a financial and administrative point – considerably easier to carry out MFT. Other issues, such as the parents taking time off work to attend MFT, are very similar in all countries. MFT that takes place for two or three hours in fortnightly or even less frequent intervals is acceptable for most working parents, particularly if sessions are held in the late afternoon. This is also a better time for children who attend school. For families with major problems and which require whole-day attendance over weeks, there may be a problem getting time off work or negotiating planned school absences. Parents may take their annual leave to be able to participate in MFT, they may work shifts or take it in turns to attend, or they may opt for getting a sickness certificate. We tend to 'co-construct' with parents the diagnosis they would like to see on such a certificate rather than merely reverting to the old-fashioned and time-honoured practices of a doctor making a 'one-way' diagnosis. Whilst we have so far refrained from handing each parent an abridged version of *DSM IV* or *ICD 10*, the temptation to do so has been there. Instead we discuss with parents a 'menu' of possible diagnoses and we have found that 'depression', 'anxiety state' and 'post-traumatic stress disorder' are much more popular self-diagnoses than 'borderline personality disorder' or 'paranoid schizophrenia'. We have found that families, if given the time and opportunity to reflect on their own states of mind, have a remarkable ability to come up with fitting and accurate diagnoses.

It is important that MFT is scheduled at 'consumer-friendly' times, for example, in the late afternoon, evening or even on weekends. This allows 'significant others', including fathers, to consider attending some of the MFT work. Clinicians need to consider, together with each family, how useful and realistic it is to expect that everybody attends each MFT. For example, teenagers, particularly if they are the sibling(s) of a problem child, will hardly want to take part in anything by the name of 'therapy'. There is little point coercing them to attend every single MFT group, but they can perhaps be encouraged to be as present during MFT as they are present in the home. It is our experience that with the average teenager, who uses home as a glorified bed and breakfast establishment, this usually does not amount to more than 10 to 15 waking hours per week. In other words, teenagers spend generally no more than ten per cent of their (waking!) time at home with their families. We therefore suggest that they should come to no more than ten per cent of the therapy time scheduled for their family. Thus, in the case of a family attending a day unit for families, the adolescent is invited to take part in the work on one out of ten days. We use a similar model for semi-absent fathers or mothers: they also are only part-time MFT attenders, thereby reflecting their seeming 'part-time status' in the family.

Ground rules

All institutions and work settings do have their own specific rules and regulations, some of which are written down and explicitly stated, while others are not. These can cover a whole range of issues, including confidentiality, equal opportunities, antidiscriminatory practice, how to manage threats of verbal or physical violence, the use of drugs and alcohol on the premises, smoking indoors, health and safety issues, and so on. Clinicians need to take these rules and regulations into account wherever they carry out their work, be that in schools, clinics, social services offices, inpatient units or private settings. Furthermore, clinicians are also guided by the rules that their own professional organizations have laid down. In institutions we often come across statements, usually couched in official and bureaucratic language, that violation of or non-compliance with existing rules and regulations leads to removal of clients from the premises and/or exclusion from therapeutic work. Such stark, if not rigid, officialdom is in strong contrast to the belief system of many therapists that one should make therapeutic use of the making and breaking of rules and regulations. There is a tension between institution-specific rules and the rules established in the course of MFT work – and this generates plenty of dilemmas which need to be made transparent to and be shared with all the families.

In MFT, as in other applications of systemic therapy, we prefer to co-construct or co-develop the rules and regulations that should govern the work. Instead of facing our clients with a barrage of 'dos' and 'don'ts' at the start, group participants are asked, within the first days of the work: 'What do you think should be the ground rules of this work?' This is not a one-off question and discussion but should open up an ongoing discussion, with 'old' rules being questioned and different ones introduced as new situations arise and new experiences are made. Since it is a major ingredient and aim of MFT for clients to use their own resources, their ideas on what the rules are have to be of major importance.

A major issue that is usually brought up spontaneously by families and their individual members has to do with confidentiality and boundary issues. MFT, like any other form of group work or therapy, raises very specific confidentiality issues. The building of mutual trust is essential when wanting to share sensitive personal information with other families and their individual members. Unlike therapists who are bound by well-established professional confidentiality codes, clients are under no such obligations. Yet, opening up to others is essential when wanting to compare experiences and the fear of sensitive information 'getting out' can inhibit people. To address this issue, one of the 'rules' that is agreed at the outset is that nobody should talk about anything they do not want to talk about and that each person is responsible for what personal information they disclose in a group setting. In other words, nobody should feel coerced to talk about what they do not wish to talk about. Therapists can also raise the question whether all group members should sign a piece of paper which would commit them not to talk about the group outside the boundaries. For some MFT practitioners this is a 'must', for others the given word counts as much as a signature on a piece of paper which has little legal clout. Clearly confidentiality is an issue that benefits most from discussion and reflection rather than merely laying down the law. Confidentiality issues can be thematized via a group exercise called 'Chinese Whispers' (this is not, as many other potential exercises, included on our 'menu' of MFT exercises as by now readers will have acquired the skills to invent or adapt their own exercises). Confidentiality can be a particular issue for families who have known each other prior to starting MFT or who live in the same neighbourhood, or in small and closely knit communities where allegedly 'everybody knows everybody'. Hence there is acute concern about others in the area finding out that they are 'mad' or 'bad'. This can be a justified initial fear and it helps to explore rather than dismiss it. Children also need to be involved in these discussions, with their parents, as MFT confidentiality issues frequently mirror issues to do with what one keeps 'in the family', and what is allowed to go out and what not. Children can be invited to think about what, if anything, they would wish their own friends in school to know about what went on in MFT. They are asked to put themselves in the shoes of other children in the group and how they might feel if something about their personal life was gossiped about in school.

MFT therapists themselves often struggle with confidentiality issues, given that they are told 'confidential' information in individual or single family meetings which are not meant to be shared with the wider group. It can be difficult for family workers to remember what is meant to be 'public' knowledge and what not. Exploring with a family, or an individual member, why certain pieces of information cannot or must not be disclosed to others is important and clarifies matters for the family and for the family worker.

Another issue that is often raised has to do with 'bad language' and swearing – particularly in front of children. This may also include verbal abuse and threatened physical violence. All institutions have policies, and the question is whether one uncompromisingly adheres to these or whether one allows these to be questioned and discussed. Merely suppressing or excluding bad or unacceptable behaviours and those who display these is one solution and can help to provide a sanitized and orderly setting. However, it also misses the chance of working with what are 'bread and butter' experiences for many families. Having them 'enacted' in the MFT setting allows working with them rather than merely banning bad behaviours from the premises. However, this can at times be a very complicated path to negotiate, as not raising and challenging unacceptable communications or behaviours may be construed by families as staff tolerating or indeed welcoming them. Physical violence should never be tolerated, but on the very rare occasions when it happens it is better to work with its impact on everybody rather than merely excluding the perpetrators. In all the years of our work in MFT we have never seen people getting physically hurt: after all it is a public context in which people are on 'best' (or least bad) behaviour. Drug or alcohol intoxication on the premises is of course also not on. On the occasion when a parent attends in an intoxi-cated state, we ask whether it is safe for them to parent their child(ren). The metaphor of 'driving whilst over the limit' is utilized to ask all families pres-ent whether there should be a 'parenting licence', and if so whether it should be taken away or be temporarily suspended. We also make use of a breath-alyzer to test the actual alcohol levels, and if the person shows unacceptable levels (i.e. 0.1 per cent or above), the parent is asked to leave the premises and to return when sober. Smoking is not allowed in public buildings in the United Kingdom nor in many other parts of the world. Adults tend to smoke outside if they need to and have their dependent children minded by a responsible adult whilst they do.

The exercise 'The Ten Family Commandments' can be adapted by all the families attending MFT to 'The Ten Group Commandments', with discus-sions as to how these can be enforced. There are clearly quite a few potential issues that one could 'legislate' about and if families do not raise these therapists may ask whether some of the following might be relevant: use of mobile phones and computer games; cleanliness and tidiness (who clears up whose mess?); racist, sexist and other discriminatory remarks and behaviours; responsibility for own children's behaviours; attendance of family friends or acquaintances; health and safety issues; 'talking and listening' rules; time-keeping. If any of these issues is not put 'on the map' by the families them-selves, the therapists can flag up some of those missed out: 'Do you think we need to think about what happens if . . .?' One can also encourage discussion on any sanctions if specific rules are broken and whether sanctions the first time round should be different from those dished out on subsequent occa-sions. Involving the families in devising rules and sanctions enables their own sense of agency. It is extremely rare that the rules made are in straight conflict with institutional rules, but if this happens the therapists can confront the families with this dilemma and ask for ideas to resolve it.

The recording of MFT sessions, by video or DVD, can also raise various confidentiality issues. In some settings any recording is seen as a health record and needs to be preserved for 25 years. This is particularly complicated when recordings of whole groups, with different families and individuals all in the same frame, are concerned. This policy is clearly nonsense when applied to MFT work as the recording cannot be regarded as the 'medical record' of just one client (or family). We tend to conceive of audiovisual recording made during MFT as mere therapeutic tools, aimed at helping families to benefit from feedback and to look at themselves from a different perspective, so as to assist them to make some of the required changes. At the end of the specific MFT work, the recordings are therefore wiped out. From a legal point of view, it is essential that families give written consent to being filmed. Such consent is not always easy to obtain, as there are individuals and families who simply resist this idea. Many of them change their minds after a while, after observing the benefits other families derive from video feedback sessions. However, some families or their individual members refuse to be filmed and this may result in complicated arrangements so they can be kept 'out of the frame' when sessions are recorded.

MFT training

Over the past few years formal MFT trainings have been developed in various countries, including the UK and Germany, as well as in the USA and Canada (Raasoch and Laqueur 1979; Saayman *et al.* 2006). Prior to this, systemic therapists had learned MFT by participant observation during their placements with experienced teams. This apprenticeship model then led to clinicians transferring their newly learned skills and experiences to their own specific work settings. Many of the existing MFT projects came into being in this way and they often relied on energetic clinicians with the determination to implement the approach, with considerable 'trial and error' experiences.

MFT concepts and techniques can be taught in a relatively short time to systemically trained clinicians, with reinforcement of the previous *conceptual* training in the systems therapies, as well training in *perceptual* skills particularly relevant for MFT (Saayman *et al.* 2006). MFT trainings focus specifically on the acquisition of skills that promote cross-family linkage and also concern themselves with managing inter-family interactions between subgroups and families (McFarlane *et al.* 1993), so that families and their individual members can become 'co-workers'. Another major aspect of training is to help clinicians to have confidence in the families' own resources and to see it as their task to help families and their individual members to (re)discover these. This is much easier said than done, as it goes against the traditional trainings most mental health professionals receive. Learning 'not to be too helpful', not to provide quick answers and solutions, not to be the expert, learning to wait for other ideas to emerge – all this takes some unlearning of patterns which the 'helping' professions have previously acquired. Using creative and playful working methods does not come easily to professionals for whom 'play' and the allegedly 'serious business of therapy' have been incompatible bedfellows.

The format and intensity of MFT training depends very much on the prior experience of trainee clinicians. For example, the Marlborough Family Service offers a nine-month programme for systemically trained therapists. This begins with a two-day, practically oriented familiarization with the basic principles and techniques of MFT. Here simulated MFT role plays which focus on the positioning of the therapist are a central teaching tool. The participation in these initial two 'taster' days, which are held three times a year, is a prerequisite for further training. Over the following nine months there are three blocks of two full days during which the application of MFT to specific work settings and client groups is discussed and developed. Course participants have to be involved in actual MFT work, already ongoing or at least about to emerge. This allows the training to be 'hands on' and informed by practice rather than merely being a 'dry run'. As the courses are attended by clinicians from quite diverse work settings, there is the potential for a lot of cross-fertilization. In fact, the training itself embodies the ethos and principles of MFT, with the large group of individual teams ('professional families') sharing their experiences, inspiring and learning from each other. Between the three training blocks, there is specific institution-based work, in the form of ongoing supervision and consultation. This tends to be on a twice monthly basis and, depending on geography, can take the form of direct face-to-face consultation and supervision, or for this to take place via email, viewing of videotape segments and reading written accounts.

We are aware that 'first generation' MFT projects often developed via trial and error, but increasingly we think that, now that there is a lot of expertise in different teams all over the world, formal training programmes, as described above, are essential to promote the emergence of high quality MFT projects, accompanied by ongoing supervision and consultation. We are concerned that professionals who have no prior systemic training – for example, teachers who 'adopt' the Marlborough model of the 'Family Class' – use MFT techniques and concepts in a rather linear way, without considering the often complex contextual issues and the need for other simultaneous interventions. MFT clinicians need to have the systemic skills of being trained context readers, context makers and context managers. As families participating in MFT graduate from learners to experts, so do trainee clinicians, and they can then use their expertise to develop further multi-family groups, jointly with graduate families, with a close tie-in to the broader helping system.

Language barriers and bridges

Can families participate in MFT if they do not speak the 'dominant' language? The answer to this often raised question is a wholehearted 'yes'. However, it needs to be added that this can prove difficult, at least at the outset. It may seem an odd idea to have a number of interpreters working alongside families in a large MFT group. If, for example, two or three families do not speak English and, to make it more complicated, they each speak a specific minority language, then there may be four parallel languages spoken in the same room. How can everybody be heard and respected in such a 'Tower of Babel'? The work requires a lot of patience and tolerance on everybody's part as every sentence uttered by family members will need to be translated backwards and forwards into each of the languages. In order for this to work, high levels of respect and self-discipline are required, as everyone has to wait until the interpreters have finished their translation. Most families find this very laborious at the beginning, as it slows down the group process, and it is not at all uncommon for 'native' English speakers to challenge 'foreign' families openly and question families as to why they 'still haven't learned to speak English? How long have you been here?' It is only over time that the 'otherness' becomes intriguing, that English-speaking families want to tune into the different sounds and the related experiences and cultural values. It is our experience that over time almost all families acquaint each other with 'the other' and say they feel enriched by the cultural diversity they have encountered. An MFT exercise, 'Tower of Babel', can help to facilitate this process. Here everybody, including native English speakers, is asked to talk in some ancient and now utterly incomprehensible 'fantasy' language. The aim is to make themselves understood to everybody in the room. A specific task or exercise is set (see Chapters 3–5), and this has to be carried out without using English or any other recognizable language. Some family members can become 'ad hoc interpreters' and guess what specific communications mean. The person or persons whose utterances have been 'translated' can non-verbally signal whether this translation is correct or not. Afterwards the whole group can discuss and compare their experiences and relate these to their position, not only in the group but also in society or when visiting a country where they cannot speak the language.

Whilst interpreters are needed for families to communicate with each other, they can also get in the way and literally act as barriers between families. This is particularly the case if they are around for the whole duration of MFT groups as they often talk with their allocated family and thereby impede naturally evolving interactions between families. In practice, we ask interpreters to be present for specific discussion groups, perhaps a planning or reflections meeting, or when discussing what people made of a specific exercise. We often ask interpreters to assume a participant observer position, at some physical distance from 'their' family; their ideas and perspectives, not only on 'their' family but also on others, can be helpful and complementary.

Contraindications to MFT

MFT is often used in combination with other therapeutic interventions and not as a stand-alone approach. It is also a work context within which other interventions can be made, with individual, couple and single family sessions. When families are first told about having therapy together with other families, they tend to be sceptical: washing one's dirty linen in public is not something most people want to do. Hence, there are families who will reject the idea of taking part in such work. This is an entirely natural reaction but not a reason for excluding these families from the work. It very much depends on who tells them what it is all about and this is where ex-service users can be very helpful. We also know that many families who feel initially coerced, by social services or courts, to participate in assessment programmes which are MFT-based quickly become converted to seeing the advantages of this approach. Furthermore, they can be helped to understand the model by attending introductory evenings and meeting other families. In this sense initial reluctance is not a contraindication to MFT. Clients with acute psychotic disturbances should also not participate in MFT groups because of the serious disruption they can cause. The same is the case for highly dependent substance misusers. We have also found that it is very difficult to undertake MFT work with an anorectic teenager if her mother is herself seriously anorectic.

If there is one group of clients who cannot participate in MFT, it is men or women who are suspected or convicted sexual abusers or paedophiles. Allowing them to attend MFT involving families with young children gives them easy access to new targets. Therapists soon turn into 'social policemen' in their efforts to provide high levels of surveillance in their wish to protect children. Meeting vulnerable women and their dependent children is a particular attraction for sexually deviant men. If they refuse to disclose or if they altogether deny their sexual bias, therapists may have to tell other families so that they can adequately protect their children during the therapeutic work. This does of course break confidentiality rules, even if it is in the interests of other children in the group. As a result, there is little trust in the group with increasing levels of suspicion, surely not the basis for developing close and mutually trusting relationships with other families. Furthermore, a therapist who feels the need to police MFT is usually not creative. Whilst it is possible to work with sexual abusers in other settings, this is not the case with MFT. This is different from working with families where there is a lot of domestic violence or other forms of physical and emotional abuse. The Marlborough Family Service has over the past 33 years worked with thousands of families presenting with intra-familial emotional and physical violence and to date there have not been any physical fights between, or injuries to, any of the families. Finally, another exclusion category from MFT are adults or teenagers who have committed violent extra-familial crimes, simply because of the risk they pose to the families on the premises.

The future of MFT

This book may seem somewhat biased – biased in favour of describing the merits of working in multiple contexts with multiple families, continuously generating multiple perspectives. Whilst professional bias can be inspiring, it also has serious disadvantages and thus needs to be placed in context. We can categorically state that whilst we are fans of the approach, MFT must not be idealized: the one thing MFT has in common with all other psychotherapies is that it does not perform miracles. It can be useful as a stand-alone approach, but it is generally more useful in combination with other therapies and treatment approaches. However, combined treatments are much more difficult to evaluate than 'pure' treatments, as these need to be evaluated first before 'hybrid' therapies can be put to the test. In this book we have described how MFT can be a powerful mode of treatment that assists other treatment approaches, such as the medical, behavioural and psychotherapeutic regimes developed for patients with schizophrenia. With other client groups, it may play a major part in the overall intervention, as in the case of work with multiproblem families. MFT day programmes provide intensive in vivo experiences that are more likely to bring about changes in 'stuck' and chronically help-seeking families than the more traditional single family therapy approaches. However, even with intensive multi-family day programmes, other interventions have to be carried out simultaneously, such as individual, couple and single family work.

Clinicians who consider using MFT are well advised to start using the approach with what appear to be the 'easier' families, in other words families which are not too disturbed. One also has to keep in mind that there is a considerable risk that whenever one promotes a new approach and invites referrals, particularly from sceptical colleagues, one tends to receive the most 'impossible' cases. MFT is unlikely to work when everything else has failed. We recommend that clinicians start with small and discrete MFT projects, initially funded from existing resources rather than making a plea for up-front pump-prime funding – which is usually not forthcoming. Using the financial argument as an excuse for being unable to start MFT is not uncommon but hardly credible, particularly if one considers that two staff can treat six to eight families at the same time. A pilot project can encourage staff to acquire confidence and competencies and it can also serve to convince colleagues and managers at a later stage to invest in MFT. At the outset it is best not to replace an already existing project by a new MFT venture, as institutional resistance(s) may give it a bad start. MFT should rather be thought of as an 'add-on', there to assist already good work rather than being perceived as a potential competitor.

This book has described evolving work in this field and we hope that it can contribute to the growth of new projects which help families and their individual members to be better places to live in – and with.

References

Abrahams, J. and Varon, E. (1953) *Maternal Dependency and Schizophrenia: Mothers and Daughters in a Therapeutic Group. A Group Analytic Study*. New York: International Universities Press.

Andersen, T. (1987) The reflecting team. *Family Process* 26, 415–428.

Anderson, C.M. (1983) A psychoeducational program for families of patients with schizophrenia. In W. R. McFarlane (ed.) *Family Therapy in Schizophrenia*. New York: Guilford Press.

Anderson, C.M., Griffin, S., Rossi, A., Pagonis, I., Holder, D. and Treiber, R. (1986) A comparative study of the impact of education vs. process groups for families of patients with affective disorders. *Family Process* 25, 185–205.

Aponte, H. (1976) The family school interview: an eco structural approach. *Family Process* 15, 303–313.

Asay, T.P. and Lambert, M.J. (1999) The empirical case for the common factors in therapy: quantitative findings. In M.A. Hubble, B.L. Duncan and D.M. Scott (eds) *The Heart and Soul of Change. What Works in Therapy*. Washington DC: APA.

Asen, E. (1997) From Milan to Milan: true tales about the structural Milan approach. *Human Systems* 8, 39–42.

Asen, E. (2002) Multiple family therapy: an overview. *Journal of Family Therapy* 24, 3–16.

Asen, E. (2006) Systemic approaches – critique and scope. In S. Timimi and M. Begum (eds) *Critical Voices in Child and Adolescent Mental Health*. London: Free Association Books.

Asen, E. (2007a) Multi-contextual multiple family therapy. In L. Mayes, P. Fonagy and M. Target (eds) *Developmental Science and Psychoanalysis*. London: Karnac.

Asen, E. (2007b) Changing 'multi-problem families' – developing a multi-contextual systemic approach. In F.W. Seibel, H.-U. Otto and G. Frisenhahn (eds) *Reframing the Social – Festschrift Walter Lorenz*. Boskovice: Verlag Albert.

Asen, E. (2007c) Therapeutic assessments: assessing the ability to change. In C. Thorpe and J. Trowell (eds) *Re-rooted Lives: Interdisciplinary Work with the Family Justice System*. Bristol: Jordan Publications.

Asen, E. and Bianchi, S. (2007) DAPHNE report: The European multi-family approach. www.multifamilyassessment.net.

Asen, E. and Jones, E. (1999) Couple therapy and depression. *Context* 41, 22–23.

Asen, E. and Schmidt, U. (eds) (2005) Special issue: Multi-family therapy in anorexia nervosa. *Journal of Family Therapy* 27, 101–182.

Asen, E. and Scholz, M. (2008) Multi-Familientherapie in unterschiedlichen Kontexten. *Praxis der Kinderpsychologie und Kinderpsychiatrie* 57, 362–380.

Asen, E. and Schuff, H. (2003) Disturbed parents and disturbed families: assessment and treatment issues. In M. Goepfert, J. Webster and M. V. Seeman (eds) *Disturbed and Mentally Ill Parents and their Children.* Cambridge: Cambridge University Press.

Asen, E. and Schuff, H. (2006) Psychosis and multiple family group therapy. *Journal of Family Therapy* 28, 58–72.

Asen, E. and Tomson, P. (1992) *Family Solutions in Family Practice.* Lancaster: Quay Publications.

Asen, E., Stein, R., Stevens, A., McHugh, B., Greenwood, J. and Cooklin, A. (1982) A day unit for families. *Journal of Family Therapy* 4, 345–358.

Asen, E., George, E., Piper, R. and Stevens, A. (1989) A systems approach to child abuse: management and treatment issues. *Child Abuse and Neglect* 13, 45–57.

Asen, E., Dawson, N. and McHugh, B. (2001) *Multiple Family Therapy. The Marlborough Model and its Wider Applications.* London & New York: Karnac.

Asen, E., Tomson, D., Young, V. and Tomson, P. (2004) *10 Minutes for the Family: Systemic Practice in Primary Care.* London: Routledge.

Badaracco, J.G. (2000) *Psicoanalisis Multifamilar.* Buenos Aires: Paidos.

Barrett, P., Farrell, L., Dadds, M. and Boulter, N. (2005) Cognitive-behavioral family treatment of childhood obsessive-compulsive disorder: long-term follow-up and predictors of outcome. *Journal of the Academy of Child and Adolescent Psychiatry* 44, 1005–1014.

Behr, H. (1996) Multiple family group therapy: a group-analytic perspective. *Group Analysis* 29, 9–22.

Benningfeld, A.B. (1978) Multiple family therapy systems. *Journal of Marriage and Family Counseling* 4, 25–34.

Benoit, J.-C., Daigremont, A., Kossmann, L., Pruss, P. and Roume, D. (1980) Groupe de rencontre multifamilial dans un pavillon de malades chroniques. *Annales medico-psychologiques* 10, 1253–1259.

Berkowitz, C. and Gunderson, J.G. (2002) Multifamily psychoeducational treatment of borderline personality disorder. In W. R. McFarlane (ed.) *Multifamily Groups in the Treatment of Severe Psychiatric Disorders.* New York: Guilford Press.

Bishop, P., Clilverd, A., Cooklin, A. and Hunt, U. (2002) Mental health matters: a multi-family framework for mental health intervention. *Journal of Family Therapy* 24, 31–45.

Boas, C.V. (1962) Intensive group psychotherapy with married couples. *International Journal of Group Psychotherapy* 12, 142–153.

Bowers, G.T. and Al-Redha, M.R. (1990) A comparison of outcome with group/marital and standard/individual therapies with alcoholics. *Journal of Studies on Alcohol* 51, 301–309.

Bradley, G.M., Couchman, G.M., Perlesz, A., Nguyen, A.T., Singh, B. and Riess, C. (2006) Multiple-family group treatment for English-speaking and Vietnamese-speaking families living with schizophrenia. *Psychiatric Services* 57, 521–530.

Brennan, J.W. (1995) A short-term psychoeducational multiple family group for bipolar patients and their families. *Social Work* 40, 737–743.

Brown, G.W. and Harris, T.O. (1978) *The Social Origins of Depression: A Study of Psychiatric Disorder in Women*. London: Tavistock.

Carlson, C. (1987) Resolving school problems with structural family therapy. *School Psychology Review* 16, 457–468.

Cassano, R. (1989) Multi-family group therapy in social work practice – part I. *Social Work with Groups* 12, 3–14.

Cecchin, G. (1987) Hypothesising, circularity and neutrality revisited: an invitation to curiosity. *Family Process* 26, 405–413.

Colahan, M. and Robinson, P.H. (2002) Multi-family groups in the treatment of young adults with eating disorders. *Journal of Family Therapy* 24, 17–30.

Cook-Darzens, S. and Doyen, C. (2006) Therapie multifamiliale de l'adolescent anorexique: une experience ambulatoire. In S. Cook-Darzens *Therapies Multi-familiales*. Ramonville Saint-Agne: Editions Eres.

Cooklin, A. (2001) Introduction. In E. Asen, N. Dawson and B. McHugh (2001) *Multiple Family Therapy. The Marlborough Model and its Wider Applications*. London & New York: Karnac.

Cooklin, A. (2004) *Being Seen and Heard. DVD Training Pack*. London: Royal College of Psychiatrists.

Cooklin, A., Miller, A. and McHugh, B. (1983) An institution for change: developing a family day unit. *Family Process* 22, 453–468.

Cooperrider, D. (1990) *Appreciative Management and Leadership: The Power of Positive Thought and Action in Organisations*. San Francisco: Jossey-Bass.

Coughlin, A. and Wimberger, H.C. (1968) Group family therapy. *Family Process* 7, 37–50.

Dalley, T. (2008) I wonder if I exist? A multi-family approach to the treatment of anorexia in adolescence. In C. Case and T. Dalley (eds) *Art Therapy with Children: From Infancy to Adolescence*. London: Routledge.

Dare, C. and Eisler, I. (2000) A multi-family group day treatment programme for adolescent eating disorder. *European Eating Disorders Review* 8, 4–18.

Dawson, N. and McHugh, B. (1986) Families as partners. *Pastoral Care in Education* 4, 102–109.

Dawson, N. and McHugh, B. (1987) Talking to parents of children with emotional and behavioural difficulties. *British Journal of Special Education* 14, 119–121.

Dawson, N. and McHugh, B. (1994) Parents and children: participants in change. In E. Dowling and E. Osborne (eds) *The Family and the School: A Joint Systems Approach to Problems with Children*. London: Routledge.

Dawson, N. and McHugh, B. (2000) Family relationships, learning and teachers – keeping the connections. In R. Best and C. Watkins (eds) *Tomorrow's Schools*. London: Routledge.

Dawson, N. and McHugh, B. (2005) Multi-family groups in schools: the Marlborough model. *Context* 79, 10–12.

Dawson, N. and McHugh, B. (2006) A systemic response to school-based violence from a UK perspective. *Journal of Family Therapy* 28, 267–271.

De Shazer, S. (1982) *Patterns of Brief Therapy: An Ecosystemic Approach*. New York: Guilford Press.

Detre, T., Sayer, J., Norton, A. and Lewis, H. (1961) An experimental approach to the treatment of the acutely ill psychiatric patient in the general hospital. *Connecticut Medicine* 25, 613–619.

Döhler, I. (2008) *Die Behandlung der Anorexia nervosa im Jugendalter. Klinischer Effektivitätsvergleich zwischen Multifamilientherapie und traditioneller psychiatrischer Behandlung*. Inauguraldissertation an der Medizinischen Fakultät Carl Gustav Carus der TU Dresden.

Dombalis, A.O. and Erchul, W.P. (1987) Multiple family group therapy: a review of its applicability to the practice of school psychology. *School Psychology Review* 16, 487–497.

Dowling, E. and Osborne, E. (1985) *The Family and the School. A Joint Systems Approach to Problems with Children*. London: Routledge.

Dyck, D.G., Short, R.A., Hendryx, M.S., Norell, D., Myers, M., Patterson, T., *et al.* (2000) Management of negative symptoms among patients with schizophrenia attending multiple-family groups. *Psychiatric Services* 51, 513–519.

Dyck, D.G., Hendryx, M.S., Short, R.A., Voss, W.D. and McFarlane, W.R. (2002) Service use among patients with schizophrenia in psychoeducational multiple-family group treatment. *Psychiatric Services* 53, 749–754.

Eisler, I. (2005) The empirical and theoretical base of family therapy and multiple family day therapy for adolescent anorexia nervosa. *Journal of Family Therapy* 27, 104–131.

Eisler, I. (2006) The heart of the matter – a conversation across continent. *Journal of Family Therapy* 28, 329–333.

Eisler, I., LeGrange, D. and Asen, E. (2003) Family treatments. In J. Treasure, U. Schmidt and E. van Furth (eds) *Handbook of Eating Disorders: Theory, Treatment and Research*. Chichester: Wiley.

El Farricha, M. (2006) La therapie sociale multifamiliale: pour la promotion des familles precaires. In S. Cook-Darzens (ed.) *Therapies Multifamiliales*. Ramonville Saint-Agne: Editions Eres.

Fals-Stewart, W., Klostermann, K., Yates, B.T., O'Farrell, T.J. and Birchler, G.R. (2005) Brief relationship therapy for alcoholism: a randomized clinical trial examining clinical efficacy and cost-effectiveness. *Psychology of Addictive Behaviors* 19, 363–371.

Fals-Stewart, W., Birchler, G.R. and Kelley, M.L. (2006) Learning sobriety together: a randomized clinical trial examining behavioural couples therapy with female alcoholic patients. *Journal of Counselling and Clinical Psychology* 74, 579–591.

Faulkner, A. and Thomas, P. (2002) User-led research. *British Journal of Psychiatry* 180, 1–3.

Fraenkel, P. (2006) Engaging families as experts: collaborative family program development. *Family Process* 45, 237–257.

Frager, S. (1978) Multiple family therapy: a literature review. *Family Therapy* 5, 105–120.

Fristad, M.A., Goldberg-Arnold, J.S. and Gavazzi, S.M. (2003) Multi-family psycho-education groups in the treatment of children with mood disorders. *Journal of Marital and Family Therapy* 29, 491–504.

Geist, R., Heinmaa, M., Stephens, D., Davis, R. and Katzman, D. (2000) Comparison of family therapy and family group psychoeducation in adolescents with anorexia nervosa. *Canadian Journal of Psychiatry* 45, 173–178.

Gonzalez, S., Steinglass, P. and Reiss, D. (1989) Putting the illness in its place: discussion groups for families with chronic medical illnesses. *Family Process* 28, 69–87.

Gottlieb, A. and Pattison, E.M. (1966) Married couples group psychotherapy. *Archives of General Psychiatry* 14, 143–152.

Hardcastle, D.R. (1977) A mother–child, multi-family, counseling program: procedures and results. *Family Process* 16, 67–74.

Harter, C., Kick, J. and Rave-Schwank, M. (2002) Psychoeducational group for patients with depression and their families. *Psychiatrische Praxis* 29, 160–163.

Hazel, N.A., McDonell, M.G., Short, R.A., Berry, C.M., Voss, W.D., Rodgers, M.L., *et al.* (2004) Impact of multiple family groups for outpatients with schizophrenia on caregivers' distress and resources. *Psychiatric Services* 55, 35–41.

Holmes, S. (1982) Failure to learn: a systems view. *Australian Journal of Family Therapy* 4, 27–36.

Igodt, P. (1983) La therapie d'un groupe de familles et sa mise en practique d'apres Peter Laqueur. *Therapie familiale* 4, 81–97.

Jones, E. and Asen, E. (2000) *Systemic Couple Therapy and Depression*. London: Karnac.

Jones, M. (1968) *Social Psychiatry in Practice*. London: Pelican.

Kahn, S. and Prestwood, A.R. (1954) Group therapy of parents as an adjunct to the treatment of schizophrenic patients. *Psychiatry* 17, 177–185.

Kaufman, E. and Kaufman, P. (1979) Multiple family therapy with drug abusers. In E. Kaufman and P. Kaufman (eds) *Family Therapy of Drug and Alcohol Abuse*. New York: Gardner.

Keitner, G., Drury, L., Ryan, C., Miller, I., Norman, W. and Solomon, D. (2002) Multifamily group treatment for major depressive disorder. In W.R. McFarlane (ed.) *Multifamily Groups in the Treatment of Severe Psychiatric Disorders*. New York: Guilford Press.

Keller, F. and Schuler, B. (2002) Psychoeducational groups for families of in-patients with affective disorder – experiences with a person-oriented approach. *Psychiatrische Praxis* 29, 130–139.

Laing, R.D. (1960) *The Divided Self*. London: Tavistock.

Laing, R.D. and Esterson, A. (1964) *Sanity, Madness and the Family*. London: Tavistock.

Laqueur, H.P. (1969) Multiple family therapy in a state hospital. *Hospital and Community Psychiatry* 20, 13–20.

Laqueur, H.P. (1972) Mechanisms of change in multiple family therapy. In C.J. Sager and H. Kaplan (eds) *Progress in Group and Family Therapy*. New York: Bruner/Mazel.

Laqueur, H.P. (1973) Multiple family therapy: questions and answers. In D. Bloch (ed.) *Techniques of Family Psychotherapy: A Primer*. New York: Gruner & Stratton.

Laqueur, H.P. (1976) Multiple family therapy. In P.J. Guerin (ed.) *Family Therapy: Theory and Practice*. New York: Gardner.

Laqueur, H.P., La Burt, H.A. and Morong, E. (1964) Multiple family therapy: further developments. *Current Psychiatric Therapies* 4, 150–154.

Larner, G. (2004) Family therapy and the politics of evidence. *Journal of Family Therapy* 26, 17–39.

Leff, J. and Vaughn, C. (1985) *Expressed Emotion in Families: Its Significance for Mental Illness*. New York: Guilford Press.

Le Grange, D. and Lock, J. (2007) *Treatment Manual for Bulimia Nervosa: A Family-Based Approach*. New York: Guilford Press.

Leichter, E. and Shulman, G.L. (1974) Multiple family group therapy: a multidimensional approach. *Family Process* 13, 95–110.

Lemmens, G., Eisler, I., Heireman, M. van Houdenhove, B. and Sabbe, B. (2005) Family discussion groups with patients with chronic pain and their family members: a pilot study. *Australian and New Zealand Journal of Family Therapy* 26, 21–32.

Lemmens, G., Eisler, I., Migerode, L., Heireman, M. and Demyttenaere, K. (2007) Family discussion group therapy for depression: a brief systemic multi-family group intervention for hospitalized patients and their family members. *Journal of Family Therapy* 29, 49–68.

Lemmens, G., Eisler, I., Buysse, A., Heene, E. and Demyttenaere, K. (2009a) The effects on mood of adjunctive single family and multi-family group therapy in the treatment of hospitalized patients with major depression: a 15 months follow-up study. *Psychotherapy and Psychosomatics* 78, 98–105.

Lemmens, G., Eisler, I., Dierick, P., Lietaer, G. and Demyttenaere, K. (2009b) Therapeutic factors in a systemic multi-family group treatment for major depression: patients' and partners' perspectives. *Journal of Family Therapy* 31, 250–269.

McCrady, B.S., Paolino, T.J., Longabough, R. and Rossi, J. (1979) Effects of joint hospital admission and couples treatment for hospitalized alcoholics: a pilot study. *Addictive Behaviours* 4, 155–165.

McDonell, M.G., Short, R.A., Berry, C.M. and Dyck, D.G. (2006) Multiple-family group treatment of outpatients with schizophrenia: impact on service utilization. *Family Process* 45, 359–373.

McFarlane, W.R. (1982) Multiple family in the psychiatric hospital. In H. T. Harbin (ed.) *The Psychiatric Hospital and the Family*. New York: Spectrum.

McFarlane, W.R. (ed.) (1993) Multiple family groups and the treatment of schizophrenia. In W.R. McFarlane (ed.) *Family Therapy in Schizophrenia*. New York: Guilford Press.

McFarlane, W.R. (2002) *Multifamily Groups in the Treatment of Severe Psychiatric Disorder*. New York: Guilford Press.

McFarlane, W.R., Dunne, E., Lukens, E., Newmark, M., McLaughlin-Toran, J., Deakins, S., *et al.* (1993) From research to clinical practice: dissemination of New York state's family psychoeducation project. *Hospital and Community Psychiatry* 44, 265–270.

McFarlane, W.R., Link, B., Dushay, R., Marchall, J. and Crilly, J. (1995a) Psychoeducational multiple family groups: four year relapse outcome in schizophrenia. *Family Process* 34, 127–144.

McFarlane, W.R., Lukens, E., Link, B., Dushay, R., Deakins, S.A., Newmark, M., *et al.* (1995b) Multiple-family groups and psychoeducation in the treatment of schizophrenia. *Archives of General Psychiatry* 52, 679–687.

McHugh, B., Dawson, N., Scrafton, A. and Asen, E. (2010) Hearts on their sleeves: the use of systemic biofeedback in school settings. *Journal of Family Therapy*.

McKay, M., Harrison, M., Gonzalez, J., Kim, L. and Quintana, E. (2002) Multiple family groups for urban children with conduct difficulties and their families. *Psychiatric Services* 53, 1467–1468.

Miller, A., Rathus, J. and Linehan, M. (2007) *Dialectical Behaviour Therapy with Suicidal Adolescents*. New York: Guilford Press.

Miller, I.W., Solomon, D.A., Ryan, C.E. and Keitner, G.I. (2004) Does adjunctive family therapy enhance recovery from bipolar mood episodes? *Journal of Affective Disorders* 82, 431–436.

Miller, S.D. and Duncan, B. (2000) Paradise lost: from model-driven to client-directed, outcome-informed clinical work. *Journal of Systemic Therapies* 19, 20–35.

Minuchin, S. (1974) *Families and Family Therapy*. Cambridge MA: Harvard University Press.

Minuchin, S. and Fishman, H.C. (1981) *Family Therapy Techniques*. Cambridge MA: Harvard University Press.

Minuchin, S., Montalvo, B., Guerney, B.G., Rosman, B.L. and Schumer, F. (1967) *Families of the Slums*. New York: Basic Books.

Minuchin, S., Rosman, B.I. and Baker, L. (1978) *Psychosomatic Families: Anorexia Nervosa in Context*. Harvard: Cambridge University Press.

Moltz, D. and Newmark, M. (2002) Multifamily groups for bipolar illness. In W.R. McFarlane (ed.) *Multifamily Groups in the Treatment of Severe Psychiatric Disorder*. New York: Guilford Press.

Monti, P.M., Abrams, D.B., Binkoff, J.A., Zwick, W.R., Liepman, M.R., Nirenberg, T.D. *et al.* (1990) Communication skills training with family and cognitive behavioural mood management training for alcoholics. *Journal of Studies on Alcohol* 51, 263–270.

Murburg, M., Price, L. and Jalali, B. (1988) Huntington's disease: therapy strategies. *Family Systems Medicine* 6, 290–303.

O'Farrell, T.J., Cutter, H.S.G. and Floyd, F.J. (1985) Evaluating behavioural marital therapy for male alcoholics: effects on marital adjustment and communication from before to after treatment. *Behavior Therapy* 16, 147–167.

O'Farrell, T.J., Cutter, H.S.G., Choquette, K.A., Floyd, F.J. and Bayog, R.D. (1992) Behavioral marital therapy for male alcoholics: marital and drinking adjustment during the two years after treatment. *Behavior Therapy* 23, 529–549.

O'Farrell, T.J., Choquette, K.A., Cutter, H.S.G., Brown, E.D. and McCourt, W.F. (1993) Behavioral marital therapy with and without additional couples relapse prevention sessions for alcoholics and their wives. *Journal of Studies on Alcohol* 54, 652–666.

O'Farrell, T.J., Choquette, K.A. and Cutter, H.S.G. (1998) Couples relapse prevention sessions after behavioural marital therapy for male alcoholics: outcomes during the three years after starting the treatment. *Journal of Studies on Alcohol* 59, 357–370.

O'Shea, M. and Phelps, R. (1985) Multiple family therapy: current status and critical appraisal. *Family Process* 24, 555–582.

Omer, H. (2004) *Nonviolent Resistance – A New Approach to Violent and Self-Destructive Children*. Cambridge: Cambridge University Press.

Potter, S. (2007) Breaking down the wall – Parents' experiences of the school-based Marlborough Model. Unpublished MSc thesis. London: Birkbeck College and Institute of Family Therapy.

Raasoch, J. and Laqueur, H.P. (1979) Learning multiple family therapy through simulated workshops. *Family Process* 18, 95–98.

Rathus, J. and Miller, A. (2002) Dialectical behaviour therapy adapted from suicidal adolescents. *Suicide and Life Threatening Behaviour* 32, 146–157.

Relph, A. (1984) Intervening in the school, family and clinic triangle. *Australian Journal of Family Therapy* 15, 117–124.

Rendall, S. and Stewart, M. (2005) *Excluded from School: Systemic Practice for Mental Health and Education Professionals*. London: Routledge.

Retzlaff, R. (2008) *Spiel-Räume. Lehrbuch der systemischen Therapie mit Kindern und Jugendlichen*. Stuttgart: Klett-Cotta.

Retzlaff, R., Brazil, S. and Goll-Kopka, A. (2008) Multifamilientherapie bei Kindern mit Teilleistungsfertigkeiten. *Praxis Kinderpsychologie und Kinderpsychiatrie* 57, 346–361.

Rhodes, P., Baillee, A., Brown, J. and Madden, S. (2008) Can parent-to-parent consultation improve the effectiveness of the Maudsley model of family-based treatment for anorexia nervosa? A randomized control trial. *Journal of Family Therapy* 30, 96–108.

Rix, M. (2002) *Familiäre Beziehungsmuster bei psychischen Erkrankungen im Jugendalter*. Inauguraldissertation der Medizinischen Fakultät Carl Gustav Carus der TU Dresden.

Roffey, S. (2002) *School Behaviour and Families*. London: David Fulton.

Ross, W.D. (1948) Group psychotherapy with psychotic patients and their relatives. *American Journal of Psychiatry* 105, 383–386.

Saayman, V., Saayman, G. and Wiens, S. (2006) Training staff in multiple family therapy in a children's hospital: from theory to practice. *Journal of Family Therapy* 28, 404–419.

Salem, G., v Niederhäusern, O., Aubry, M. and di Giampetro, L. (1985) L'approche multifamiliale a l'hopital psychiatrique. *Archives suisses de neurology et psychiatrie* 136, 67–71.

Schemmel, H., Selig, D. and Janschewk-Schlesinger, R. (2008) *Kunst als Ressource in der Therapie*. Tübingen: dgvt-Verlag.

Schmidt, U. and Asen, E. (2005) Does multi-family day treatment hit the spot that other treatments cannot reach? *Journal of Family Therapy 27*, 101–103.

Scholz, M. and Asen, E. (2001) Multiple family therapy with eating disordered adolescents: concepts and preliminary results. *European Eating Disorders Review 9*, 33–42.

Scholz, M., Asen, E., Gantchev, K., Schell, B. and Süß, U. (2002) Familientagesklinik in der Kinderpsychiatrie: Das Dresdner Modell – Konzept und erste Erfahrungen. *Psychiatrische Praxis* 29, 125–129.

Scholz, M., Rix, M., Scholz, K., Gantchev, K. and Thömke, V. (2005) Multiple family therapy for anorexia nervosa: concepts, experiences and results. *Journal of Family Therapy* 27, 132–141.

Schweitzer-Rothers, J. (2006) Elterliche Sorgen lindern: Sprechchöre und Zeitlinienresien in der Elternberatung. In C. Tsirigotis, A. v. Schlippe and J. Schweitzer-Rothers (eds) *Coaching für Eltern*. Heidelberg: Carl-Auer.

Selvini Palazzoli, M., Boscolo, L., Cecchin, G. and Prata, G. (1980) Hypothesizing–circularity–neutrality: three guidelines for the conductor of the session. *Family Process* 19, 3–12.

Singh, R. (2000) A retrospective clinical audit of the families who attended the family day unit between 1997–1999. Unpublished MSc thesis. London: Birkbeck College and Institute of Family Therapy.

Slagerman, M. and Yager, J. (1989) Multiple family group treatment for eating disorders: a short term program. *Psychiatric Medicine* 7, 269–284.

Steinglass, P. (1998) Multiple family discussion groups for patients with chronic medical illness. *Families, Systems and Health* 16, 55–70.

Stevens, A., Garriga, X. and Epstein, C. (1983) Proximity and distance: a technique used by family day unit workers. *Journal of Family Therapy* 5, 295–305.

Strelnick, A.H. (1977) Multiple family group therapy: a review of the literature. *Family Process* 16, 307–325.

Summer, J. (1998) Multiple family therapy: its use in the assessment and treatment of child abuse. A pilot study. Unpublished MSc thesis. London: Birkbeck College and Institute of Family Therapy.

Süß-Falkenberg, U. (2005) *Familientagesklinische Behandlung bei sozial und emotional gestörten Kindern. Eine 1½ Jahres Katamnese.* Inauguraldissertation der Medizinischen Fakultät Carl Gustav Carus der TU Dresden.

Thömke, V. (2005) *Tagesklinische Multifamilientherapie bei Kindern und Jugendlichen mit Anorexia nervosa. Die Veränderung der familiären Beziehungen unter Einbeziehung der Gewichtsentwicklung, der Zufriedenheit und des Erfolgs der Behandlung.* Inauguraldissertation der Medizinischen Fakultät Carl Gustav Carus der TU Dresden.

Tomm, K. (1988) Interventive interviewing: Part III. Intending to ask lineal, circular, strategic and reflexive questions. *Family Process* 27, 1–15.

Tucker, B.Z. and Dryson, E. (1976) The family and the school: utilizing human resources to promote learning. *Family Process* 15, 125–141.

Wamboldt, M. and Levin, L. (1995) Utility of multifamily psychoeducational groups for medically ill children and adolescents. *Family Systems Medicine* 13, 151–161.

White, M. (1997) *Narratives of Therapists' Lives.* Adelaide: Dulwich Centre Publications.

White, M. and Epston, D. (1990) *Narrative Means to Therapeutic Ends.* New York: Norton.

Wooley, S. and Lewis, K. (1987) Multi-family therapy within an intensive treatment program for bulimia. In J. Harkaway (ed.) *Eating Disorders: The Family Therapy Collections.* Rockville: Aspen.

Yalom, I. (1995) *The Theory and Practice of Group Psychotherapy*, 4th edn. New York: Basic Books.

Index

Page references in *italic* indicate Tables or Figures. MFT stands for multi-family therapy.